The Children
You Teach

Susan Engel

The Children You Teach

∘∘∘∘∘∘∘∘∘∘∘∘∘∘∘∘∘∘∘∘∘

USING A DEVELOPMENTAL FRAMEWORK
IN THE CLASSROOM

HEINEMANN
Portsmouth, NH

Heinemann
361 Hanover Street
Portsmouth, NH 03801–3912
www.heinemann.com

Offices and agents throughout the world

Library of Congress Cataloging-in-Publication Data
Name: Engel, Susan L., author.
Title: The children you teach : using developmental science in the classroom
    / by Susan Engel.
Description: Portsmouth, NH : Heinemann, [2018] | Includes bibliographical
    references.
Identifiers: LCCN 2018023021 | ISBN 9780325098173
Subjects: LCSH: Child development.
Classification: LCC LB1115 .E495 2018 | DDC 372.21—dc23
LC record available at https://lccn.loc.gov/2018023021

Acquisitions Editor: Zoë Ryder White
Production Editor: Sean Moreau
Cover Designer: Suzanne Heiser
Interior Designer: Monica Ann Crigler
Typesetter: Valerie Levy, Drawing Board Studios
Manufacturing: Steve Bernier

Printed in the United States of America on acid-free paper
22 21 20 19 18 PAH 1 2 3 4 5

This book is dedicated
to my wonderful students
at Williams College.

CONTENTS

Acknowledgments xi

Prologue xiii

CHAPTER ONE What Did Aida Want? 1

Motivation ★ Engagement ★ Social Development

How Smart Do Children Need to Be? 3

What Does It Mean to Do Well? 8

CHAPTER TWO Do Children Learn to Think in School? 17

Cognition: Part One ★ Skill Acquisition ★ Major Theories
of Development

The Dawn of Thinking 21

Children Think with Their Bodies and Their Words 22

The Expanding Repertoire of Mental Tools 26

Children Do Not Develop on Their Own 27

A Quick Sketch of Intellectual Development 29

Learning to Do School 30

What Kinds of Thinking Do Children Learn in School? 32

Workbooks Versus Thinking 35

An Example of How Teachers Can Build on Children's Intuition 36

The Singular Power of Writing 37

A Shift from Skills to Problem-Solving 42

CHAPTER THREE Was Grace Lonely? 47

Friendships ★ Peer Rejection and Neglect ★ Social Development

The ABCs of Friendship 53

Boys and Girls 55

Friendship 101 59

Bullying: A Natural Behavior That Can Become a Problem 60

Classrooms That Foster Kindness 63

Quirky Social Lives 67

CHAPTER FOUR Harry's Math Problem 70

Play ⋆ Learning ⋆ Cognition: Part Two ⋆ Learning How to Learn

Play: The Foundation of Academics 73

Work and Play Reversed 74

Implicit Versus Explicit Learning 77

Reflection: The Turbo Power 80

A Bridge for Harry 82

CHAPTER FIVE Sometimes It's Good to Tiptoe 84

Attachment and Separation ⋆ Teacher-Student Interactions ⋆ Parent-Child Interactions

Four Types of Parenting 87

Connect, Connect, Connect 90

Development Is Not Solitary 94

Seeing the World Together 96

Love in the Classroom 98

Even Subtle Connections Have an Impact 101

CHAPTER SIX Charlie and Marley 103

Emergence of the Self ⋆ Self-Control ⋆ Self-Expression

Charlie: Upbeat and Out of Control 103

Marley: Too Calm? 105

What Does It Really Mean to Have Self-Control? 107

What Marshmallows Can Tell Us 110

The Reluctant Crawl Toward Self-Control 111

Marshmallow Resisters 112

The Hidden Rewards of Waiting 113

Can Self-Control Be Trained? 114

Mysterious Marley 118

How Children Become Themselves: The Self in Self-Control 119

Children Play Their Way to a Sense of Self 122

A New Perspective 124

To Fix a Problem, Start by Understanding 126

CHAPTER SEVEN Wrong School for Audrey? 128

Poverty ∗ Cognition: Part Three ∗ Literacy

The Iron Grip of Poverty 129

John Watson's Return 133

Routines: A Cognitive Foundation 138

The Home–School Connection 142

Literacy from A to Z 144

The Last Straw 151

EPILOGUE Child Development: A User's Manual 152

Guidelines for Making Changes 157

References 159

Acknowledgments

First and foremost, I thank the many teachers who have told me their stories and graciously invited me into their classrooms to observe them in action. Teaching well is one of the most challenging, exhausting, and intricate kinds of work that exists, right up there with brain surgery. Talking openly to outsiders and allowing them to watch you and your students is essential to good practice, and it is also brave. By the same token, I thank the many parents who have opened up to me and shared the pleasures and agonies of watching their children's ups and downs. I also want to thank all the developmental psychologists whose work has influenced me, some but not all of whom are cited in these pages. Though often technical, seemingly obscure, and sometimes complex, and though not always conducted for the purpose of classroom applications, their experiments, studies, and findings offer untold riches for those of us interested in what happens to children in schools.

I thank my students at Williams College. I love them, and I love talking with them about developmental psychology, children, teachers, and schools. Many of these chapters started in lectures for my courses and reflect the conversations that ensued with my students. I particularly thank Anna DeLoi, who read an early draft of this book and gave me terrific feedback.

Finally, I thank my editor, the delightful Zoë Ryder White. I learned over the course of this project that she loves writers and writing as much as she does children and teachers. What a combo, and what a privilege for someone like me.

Prologue

To be a good teacher, you need to be smart, energetic, and knowledgeable, and you need to really like kids. But that's not enough. The best teachers are also genuinely *interested* in children: what they feel, how they think, and who they are. I don't mean merely an interest in the particular lives and quirks of your particular students, though that is wonderful. I mean a curiosity about what makes children tick—how and why they change as they grow.

I taught young children well before I studied them. When I was practically still a child myself, I was hired as an assistant in a summer program for children ages three to eight. I discovered I was good at it. And I loved it. I was one of those lucky people who, as my grandmother used to say, had a way with kids. Even though I was just a teenager, I knew how to take charge, and children were drawn to me. We came to life around one another.

But even so, when my college advisor urged me to take a course in developmental psychology, I resisted. Sure, I loved teaching, and would probably teach again, but why should I study it? That seemed so pedantic. I just liked *doing* it. I didn't need to cover over my natural feel for kids with a lot of jargon and data. Then, in my sophomore year, I took a course on language development. It changed my life. I was transfixed by studies that examined children's thought processes, identified the mechanisms by which they learned to talk, and explained how their abilities changed over time. I loved the cleverness of the experiments. Stories about children that might, at one time, have seemed merely cute or simply mundane suddenly became fascinating. A two-year-old who opened and closed her mouth after watching a box open and shut was taking a first step in her effort to represent the world around her? A three-year-old who announced that the written number six was cheerful was laying the groundwork for understanding metaphors? A four-year-old who realized that the number of soup bowls he was setting out corresponded to the number of people eating dinner was discovering an important mathematical principle? I couldn't get enough of it.

Competing theories about child development riveted me. Should we be more focused on what children have in common (for instance, the ability to talk and an interest in how adults behave), or should we pay more attention to the ways in which they differ (for instance, some children are shy and others extremely gregarious, some leap at abstract problems while others are rooted in the concrete)? Did development unfold in a straight and predictable line, or did the sequence depend on a child's upbringing? Would it be more accurate to say that children's minds undergo major transformations or that they simply learn more and more as they get older? Could you separate children's emotional lives from their intellect?

And what about all those cool experiments? Babies watch a film in which a duck swims toward a curtain. The duck disappears behind the curtain. After a few seconds, two ducks emerge from behind the curtain. As the babies watch, researchers measure their heartbeats and discover the rate changes, suggesting the babies are surprised when a second duck appears. This shows that babies have an instinct for addition. I found it so intriguing to think about what it took to get inside a young child's mind. I was hooked and decided that I would be a developmental psychologist.

There was one thing I adamantly rejected during those first years of my love affair with developmental psychology: I refused to think that my work as a teacher, something I had done with ease and by instinct, had anything to do with my new skills as a social scientist. Studying children and working with them remained two separate parts of my life. During my last two years of college, I taught part-time in two public schools in New York City. Meanwhile, at college, I carried out experiments looking at how children used metaphors, and I wrote papers on important shifts in children's emotional lives. But in my mind, teaching in those two schools and the psychological research I was doing in college had nothing to do with one another.

After college, I went straight on to graduate school so that I could keep doing the work I now felt was my life's calling: developmental research. Two things happened in graduate school that changed my thinking forever.

The first was a dawning insight, rather than a sudden light bulb. I spent my mornings recording moms and their toddlers at breakfast to find out how children learn the meanings of words. Meanwhile, I spent my afternoons earning extra income by teaching at an elementary school which was across the park from my campus. All week I shuttled back and forth between studying in grad school and teaching in elementary school. In my graduate program we read research, designed new experiments, analyzed data, and argued about theories. In the elementary school teachers shared insights about how to get the kids to behave, what kinds of books sixth graders should read, and how to set up a good science project for little kids. It began to seem crazy to me that those two worlds were so disconnected.

My professors—all active researchers—rarely stepped inside a classroom. When they did, it was only to pull "subjects" out for an experimental session. More typically, graduate students collected the data, which meant that the actual living, breathing kids were only data points on a graph to the people writing the scientific papers.

The same was true in reverse. The teachers I worked with were smart and really loved kids. But they seemed to know little about current research—its methods or findings—and equally little about the processes and mechanisms that had shaped the students they dealt with. I could see that it hampered them; they had to rely on hunches, old habits that might or might not really work, advice that was good only some of the time, and whatever rules had been established by the administration. They were particularly vulnerable to pressure from parents. When a mom insisted that her kindergartner should be doing more challenging language arts, the teacher had little information to bolster *her* approach as she explained that it would be better for the little girl to spend more time playing than to complete sentences on a worksheet. I began to feel an urgent need to get these two smart, knowledgeable groups of people to talk to one another.

The second thing that changed my thinking occurred in my final year of graduate school, when I had my first child. The moment Jake was born, the worlds of teaching and research were transformed. I suddenly took all of it personally. Some of the things Jake did were uncannily like the research I had read. He sobbed with sadness when I left him with someone else. I understood why. He used both feet and his hands in an endless string of experiments, trying to make a shiny crib toy wiggle. I knew he was learning first lessons about causality. However, at other times he did things that totally contradicted the research. Though easily startled by new people who came into his orbit, he was not consistent, as the literature predicted. Instead he treated new foods, new machines, and new animals like old friends.

Theories that had intrigued me in a scholarly way now came to life as I watched my little boy crawl, put things in his mouth, watch the world around him, and change in surprising ways. But very soon that also altered the way I thought about the children I taught. They were complex, vulnerable, and roiling with inner lives— full persons, with lives far richer and more dynamic than was visible through my daily encounters with them in the classroom. I kept thinking of a line from an Anne Tyler book, about a woman who has just given birth to her first child and keeps looking around with wonder at each person she passes on the street, thinking, "That person was *born*" (1988). I now kept looking at kids in my classroom and thinking, "You are not just my student. You are a *person with a psychological history*. You were a baby once. You nursed or you drank from a bottle. Perhaps you cried a lot, or maybe you were as calm as the Dalai Lama. When you leave my classroom each day, perhaps your mind is teaming with ideas from the book I read aloud to you. Or maybe school disappears from your thoughts the minute you walk out the door, crowded with things more important to you." Suddenly it seemed imperative to me to connect real children with theories and studies from developmental psychology.

After graduate school I took a job as a full-time classroom teacher. Eventually I returned to academic life, teaching at a college. And I had two more children.

Meanwhile, more and more of my students asked me to talk about education as well as development. I had stumbled upon an opportunity to teach future teachers that no plan book, curriculum guide, or snazzy set of rules and techniques could replace the power and utility of thinking about children from a developmental perspective.

Now, whenever I give talks to teachers, I emphasize the power of a developmental perspective. Invariably, people come up to me afterward and say something like, "I get it. You convinced me. Understanding children's development will help me. So, what should I read?" And I find myself standing there with my mouth slightly open, at a total loss, not sure what to suggest. I can think of books on intellectual development and books on friendships. I can think of books comparing different cultures and books on children's emotional problems. I can think of books about toddlers and books about five- to seven-year-olds. But I can't think of one book that connects all these strands in a way that teachers would find useful. It's worse when I try to think of specific scientific articles. Each is, by necessity, so narrowly focused and technical that it can't possibly help a busy teacher. Often the particular results, attained in a lab under precise conditions, shrink to almost nothing when applied to real children in noisy, complicated, real-life settings. Those articles are written for other researchers. They don't say much that feels directly relevant to the issues that teachers face each day. The pages that follow are my attempt to fill that void.

This book is a collection of stories about real children and teachers. But it is also about children's development. Each chapter tells a story about one particular child, teacher, or classroom dilemma. No child can be understood just by thinking about one issue at a time (for instance, moral development *or* friendship). No classroom challenge can be solved only by looking at how mathematical knowledge is acquired, or by tracing the steps that lead to literacy. So, each chapter integrates several topics, which, when put together, can illuminate the classroom or the child.

The chapters are not similar to one another. Some are short; some are long. Some cover many different topics in developmental science and others zero in on just a few. Some have happy endings. A few do not. Some highlight the impressive ingenuity and insight of teachers, and others describe the missteps even the best teachers can make. Any teacher reading this book will identify with some of the teaching practices and might be put off by others, thinking, "I would never do that." I have described a wide range of actual teachers and approaches, not just the best ones. I think that conveys a more realistic picture of real teachers and real schools. You may encounter suggestions for approaches you've already been following for years, perhaps without knowing the developmental science that explains why they work. My goal here is not to romanticize or demonize teachers, but to provide a clear-eyed look at how the practice of good teaching can and should be based on a rich understanding of what goes on in classrooms and how children develop.

In the table of contents, along with each chapter title I mention the topics in developmental psychology that you will encounter in that story. You can read just the chapter that speaks to the issues you are concerned with. But if you read all of the chapters, I hope you will end up with more than the sum of the parts. Taken together, they are written to show how looking at children through a developmental lens can change what happens in the classroom and can transform the craft of teaching, making it better for everyone involved.

At the end of the book, I have included a user's manual. It lays out the ideas and suggestions contained in the preceding chapters, offering concrete methods for using a developmental framework to guide your teaching. This book is nothing like most of the practical guides teachers are often encouraged to use. I've included very few lists and fewer instructions. But my hope is that it will be one of the most practical and useful books you'll come across for your work as a teacher. Feel free to look at the Epilogue first, if it will make each story more helpful to you.

Once you have finished the book, I hope you will look at and interact with your students and classroom in a new way. But what I hope most is that it will help you to *think* differently about the children you teach.

CHAPTER ONE

What Did Aida Want?

———— ◆ ————

Motivation ⋆ Engagement ⋆ Social Development

AIDA WAS BEAUTIFUL, but sad-looking. At seven, she had long brown hair that was, at times, wavy and sun-burnished. However, more often it just hung down the sides of her head, limp and straggly. Her hazel eyes didn't sparkle, but sometimes, when she smiled, or cracked one of her sly, quiet jokes, her eyes lightened for just a few seconds. Then she returned to that vaguely flat look—small shoulders slightly rounded, gait reluctant. When Ms. Endicott saw the girls standing by their cubbies first thing in the morning, they leaned toward each other, telling jokes, hearing secrets, and touching one another's clothes. Aida was right in the mix. It was clear she liked the other girls and they liked her. But as she walked through the door into the second-grade classroom, a shadow seemed to fall over her. As the day went on, she'd wilt more, as if each lesson, each activity, was a greater burden than the last. And it wasn't as if leaving school lightened her load. She drooped out much the way she had drooped in.

   Most seven-year-olds still like school. If they have friends, that is. Regardless of whether they learn easily or labor over lessons, social inclusion is key. A spate of studies has shown that when you are seven or eight, feeling liked is crucial to thriving at school. Ms. Endicott knew how important friends were to her young students.

And it was obvious to anyone passing by the hallway that Aida felt liked. So that wasn't the problem.

Academics weren't an obvious problem either. Aida could read well enough. Nor was she lagging way behind in math. But she didn't appear to be making much progress either. She wobbled right on the edge of difficulty. But so did lots of kids. The academic skills required of second graders stumped many of her students at first. Ms. Endicott couldn't really put her finger on the problem.

Maybe Aida would turn a corner, once she really got to know the group, the room, and Ms. Endicott. Maybe she was just one of those kids who took a while to settle in. But by February, Aida appeared to be just as lackluster and reluctant as she had seemed in September. And her academic progress had stalled. She could write answers to questions about the books she was reading, but she always offered the bare minimum. And Ms. Endicott noticed that her sentences were cursory; she rarely chose nouns and verbs that tell you a child is eager to express her specific idea or feeling. She read a heart-wrenching story about a little boy named Sudan who was teased about his hair (*An Enchanted Hair Tale*, by Alexis Deveaux). Then she completed the sheet that Ms. Endicott used to make sure children understood what they had read and to help them learn how to reflect on literature. Next to the question, "What was the most important thing that happened to the main character?" Aida wrote, "Sudan was teased." Next to the question, "How did the main character feel when this happened?" Aida wrote, "He felt sad." Her answers were not wrong. They were perfectly adequate. But they didn't exactly jump off the page. In fact Ms. Endicott had no indication that Aida had strong feelings about anything she read. When she asked Aida outright, "So, Aida, whaddya think? Was that book *An Enchanted Hair Tale* any good?" Aida looked at her calmly and said, "Yeah, I guess." Ms. Endicott had the feeling Aida was trying, in her tactful way, to figure out the quickest way to leave the conversation.

Math was the same. Aida could add and subtract in her head, but haltingly. She could translate simple word problems into equations too, which was all Ms. Endicott was looking for at this point. But Ms. Endicott noticed that the minute there was anything the least bit unusual in a word problem, Aida came to a dead standstill, as if her mind had turned off. When Ms. Endicott looked over Aida's scores on the weekly math quizzes, she saw that Aida was hovering just above the thirtieth percentile. Ms. Endicott felt uncomfortable thinking it, but maybe Aida just wasn't particularly smart.

How Smart Do Children Need to Be?

One of the most taboo subjects in schools is intelligence. Most teachers would hesitate to say out loud that one child is very smart and another not so much. There is an implicit ethos that all children should be considered equally intelligent (though no one seems to hesitate to say that one child is more artistic than another, or that one is more athletic than another). By the same token, some teachers work on the assumption that going to school will make children smarter. Neither of these beliefs is, generally speaking, true. By and large, the data continue to confirm what most psychologists have believed ever since Alfred Binet developed the first IQ tests. Children vary in their fundamental ability to learn. At the lowest end of the continuum (below 85), children need special help and cannot be expected to function in the usual ways in school. The children who score on the highest end of the continuum (above 115) may also need special opportunities since they learn at a much faster rate than the others. This idea, though generally accepted among scientists, has had its critics.

One of the most taboo subjects in schools is intelligence.

Over the years psychologists such as Howard Gardner and Robert Sternberg have challenged the standard view of IQ. They and others have argued that intelligence cannot be captured by one number. Instead, they say people vary in the kinds of intelligence they possess. Someone may, from their perspectives, have a lot of verbal intelligence but little kinesthetic intelligence. Or someone may have a lot of "book smarts" but little practical acumen. But on the whole, the data don't support the idea that there are many kinds of intelligence. Children may *show* their intelligence in one domain more than another (one child is good with shapes, another with words, one child seems to shine in school tasks but fumble in more worldly, practical settings), and they may have exceptional talent at a certain activity without being all that smart. But talents and interests are not the same thing as intelligence.

Most researchers agree that intelligence measures are based on the speed and accuracy with which a child can learn new information and apply it in various situations. In recent years, that simple definition (and approach to measurement) has gained support from research showing that, even in infancy, children vary in how quickly they process information. Scientists can test an infant's speed of processing by measuring how long it takes each baby to get bored with looking at a particular image and turn to look at a new one. Those scores from infancy predict scores on IQ tests when the children are older. They also predict a fair amount about children's academic ability in school.

If you measured speed of processing in ten infants, and then administered a proper IQ test to them when they were eight, and gave them an SAT test when they were seventeen, the child who got the lowest score as a baby would still probably get the lowest score on the SAT, which is one way of showing that intelligence is highly stable. The data also clearly show that, by and large, intelligence is inherited (Plomin and Loehlin 1989). Two people with high IQ scores are likely to have a child with a high IQ. The same is true for parents with low IQ. Children who are adopted at birth often appear to be more similar in their intellectual capacity to their adoptive parents when they are four. But by the time they reach adolescence, they are likely to get a score more like that of their biological parents than the family they are now part of. And here we come to a complicated wrinkle that frequently muddies the discussion. It is true that children inherit much of their intellectual potential from their parents and that intelligence is quite stable. But there is a very important caveat to these two robust findings. A variety of outside factors can inhibit a child's native intelligence. These factors include malnutrition, exposure to drugs, poverty, extreme stress, sustained and pervasive racism, and schools that don't acknowledge their cultural habits and values. What this means is that, although intelligence is inherited and stable, by the time they are in school many children face disadvantages that eat away at the intellectual capacities with which they were born. To make sense of this paradox, reconsider the ten babies whose speed of processing was tested. If they were all the same race, and grew up in the same economic bracket, their rankings would likely remain the same over time. But now imagine that they are not all from the same racial groups and aren't part of the same economic bracket. Imagine instead that three of them are African American and seven are Caucasian (and that they are all growing up in the United States). As infants, one or more of the black children might score the highest of the whole group. But by the time they take the SAT tests, though the Caucasian children will remain similar in comparison to one another, the African American children might have lost ground. This is not due to any racial difference between them. It's because children grow up in unequal circumstances (Hart and Risley 1995).

Ms. Endicott knew all of that. She also knew that by definition, most kids have average intelligence, and that's all they need to be able to learn in school. Aida may not have been the Einstein of the group, but that wasn't the problem. Something told

Ms. Endicott that Aida's lowish scores did not reflect her real ability, and that her halting response to schoolwork wasn't the whole story. When she listened to Aida talking with friends, she heard a vocabulary and quick wit that signaled a perfectly smart girl. Ms. Endicott had the feeling it had less to do with her intellectual capacity and more to do with her on-off switch.

When it came to group projects, Aida usually pitched in. But she typically chose the smallest, simplest task—whatever presented the least challenge and effort. For example, in November Ms. Endicott put the kids into groups of three, and told them to design and build a new kind of vehicle that could take a person from one place to another. She gave them all kinds of materials—spools, wire, toilet paper dowels, buttons, paper, feathers, balsa wood, cardboard—and equipment—glue guns, small nails and hammers, rubber bands. She also gave them a few guidelines: they couldn't bring in any kind of motor from home, and the whole thing had to be made from scratch. Most of the kids were very excited by the project, intrigued by the possibilities, and the slight scent of competition between the groups. They plunged into the process of planning, testing, and fabrication with great zest. Aida's group wanted to build a wagon that could carry a person on land and water. The other two children in her team pitched various schemes, and argued about whether it would be a boat with wheels, or a wagon with a sail. Aida stayed silent. She kept glancing over to another group where her two best buddies were collaborating. When it came time to build the "Sailwagon," as they ended up calling it, she did the hot gluing. She was deft, and did a good job. But she left all the more complex and mentally challenging tasks to the other two. Aida was the same whenever there were team projects, —whether the projects were more conventionally academic (solving math problems together) or required some invention and creativity. When the children were asked to correct one another's work, Aida was thoughtful and careful. She seemed to enjoy the others when they worked together, but she barely attended to the actual content of the project. What she liked was being with the other kids. She liked it even more when those kids were her pals. In fact, all the fun she had with friends became a way of avoiding anything that had the whiff of learning. Ms. Endicott realized she had gathered a small collection of insights but wasn't sure what to do differently. Aida remained a mystery to her.

Sometimes at lunch in the faculty room, when teachers vented about various students, Ms. Endicott would mention Aida. One colleague told her to let it be. Aida wasn't causing any problems, and not every child could be a star at school. Another colleague suggested she spend just a few moments with Aida each day, making sure Aida felt good about herself. One day a student teacher, who periodically joined the lunchtime conversation, chimed in and asked why Ms. Endicott didn't bring the parents in and tell them she was concerned about Aida's lackluster performance. He explained to the others that he had been learning in his graduate program about how important the home-school connection was. Another teacher offered, "Her father just lost his job. They're going through a rough time at home. She may need therapy."

Ms. Endicott knew these suggestions were reasonable enough, but they didn't really hit the spot, either. She didn't think Aida was actually sad in any particular way or in response to something that had happened at home. Her sadness seemed to be subtler than that—more a way of being than a response to a temporary situation. She also didn't think Aida felt timid about her skills. She didn't lack confidence per se. Instead, it appeared to Ms. Endicott that Aida simply had little to no interest in shining at her work. And before she talked to Aida's parents, she definitely wanted to get a better sense of what made Aida tick. But she wasn't sure how to proceed. She might just keep an eye on her for a while longer.

Then one day during a second-grade team meeting, when Ms. Endicott was fretting that Aida seemed to be drifting away academically, a paraprofessional who came to help a little boy with cerebral palsy spoke up. "What is she like at recess?" The other teachers looked at him in surprise. What, Ms. Endicott thought, did recess have to do with Aida's academic progress?

Ms. Endicott had genuine affection for most students. She wasn't cuddly but the kids knew she liked being with them, and her decisive energy and clarity drew them in. She was also a master of the volatile classroom, easily quieting disputes and keeping the group on track. That wasn't all. Relatively comfortable with teaching second graders math and science, she was especially strong in language arts. She had loved English literature in college and had soaked up her M. Ed courses on language arts for elementary school children. She read a lot of children's books, used the Daily Five approach, and was quick to pick out the child who needed outside reading help. Over the years she had absorbed all kinds of particular solutions to specific problems. But faced with the subtle and murky mystery of a kid like Aida, Ms. Endicott felt unsure. Aida did not make trouble, she didn't have a reading disability, and she was neither bullied nor a bully. None of the tools Ms. Endicott had learned in graduate school, or after, fit this particular situation. So when the paraprofessional suggested watching Aida at recess, it threw Ms. Endicott for a loop. What did the paraprofessional think she could possibly see on the playground that might help her in the classroom?

Like most teachers, Ms. Endicott's knowledge of child development was cursory. What she had learned in grad school came from a textbook that simply outlined the basic stages of development and offered milestones along various dimensions: children of three begin making friends, seven-year-olds cannot think abstractly, nine-year-old girls express relational aggression, and so forth. The book had offered some neat little diagrams outlining the major areas of development and a few grids showing important benchmarks. Other teachers had generously wanted to help fix the problem. Yet none of them, including Ms. Endicott, really understood what the problem was. A few days later Ms. Endicott asked the paraprofessional why he thought she should watch Aida on the playground. He shrugged. He didn't have a lot of formal education in child development either. But his work as a paraprofessional had taught him one thing for sure. To find the particular way to help a child, you needed to know her from the front, the back, and the side. He had found that a lot of the most useful information came in bits and pieces. In fact, often he learned the most useful things about his students when he first walked into the classroom, or sat on the side, waiting for the regular lesson to end. He also had noticed that it took him a while. No one snapshot would do it. And sometimes the best information came outside of the classroom—the places where children weren't doing what they were told, but were just being themselves. He said, "You know, you've been telling us about the things Aida doesn't seem to enjoy. Why not see what you can learn about her when she's doing something she wants to do? Don't you want to get inside her head a little more?"

A light went on inside Ms. Endicott's brain. She realized she had gotten stuck using the same old information that usually guided her, even when it wasn't helping. She needed some new kinds of information. Instead of tracking Aida's grades on spelling tests and book reports, or simply noting that she was not unpopular, Ms. Endicott decided to start describing Aida at various times during the day, whenever she had a moment to take a few notes. She'd keep a little Aida book with her at all times. Whenever she had a moment, she'd write down where Aida was, whom she was with, and what she was doing. She'd also make a few notes about Aida's mood, her energy, and anything particular she overheard her say or saw her do. She kept remembering what the paraprofessional had said, laughing in a slightly self-deprecating way: "What do I know? I'm no psychologist. I just grab at bits and pieces. I never know which bit is going to tell me something new about my student."

One of Ms. Endicott's notes read, "Aida is standing in line with the other kids, waiting to go to gym. She's smiling at something the boy in front of her is saying. She makes a funny face. He laughs. I guess the kids find her witty. Her body seems so much springier than usual." Another note read, "Aida is at the table with Bailey and Joanne, answering the problems I gave them about the number line. Bailey and

Joanne are looking at their papers. Aida keeps looking down, but it doesn't seem like she's actually taking in anything because she keeps looking back up; I'm not sure what she's focused on and I don't think she is either. But just now she saw me watching her, and she bent her head toward the page. I'm going to go over and see if she needs help." A third said, "I just looked out the window. Aida is pretending to hold a mic and is doing a song and dance for some of the other kids. It looks like she's trying to be Pink. She's so saucy out there. The kids are eating it up."

She noticed that Aida was always liveliest when she was outside of the classroom. The dull look descended during lessons and work time. She also began to notice how often she urged Aida to work by reminding her that her grades could get better. That made her decide to look back at Aida's reports from the previous spring. Again and again, the comment said, "Aida needs to try harder." But what did it mean to ask a seven-year-old to try harder? And try harder at what? Ms. Endicott decided she needed to revisit what trying hard looked like in a second grader.

What Does It Mean to Do Well?

You don't need to be a psychologist to know that when children are motivated, they can overcome almost any obstacle, and that when they are not, even the brightest kids eventually flounder in one way or another. Most teachers see it every day in their classrooms. A kid who is eager to do well makes great strides. The one who could care less, or seems too tired to be bothered, falls behind.

But doing well can mean many different things to a child (and a teacher). It can entail winning, improving, executing a plan, finishing a task, or fulfilling a personal goal. It's only in recent years that psychologists have begun to tease apart the big glob we casually think of as motivation.

Research suggests that at an early age, children vary in their basic amount of drive (Plomin et al. 1993). One child seems to have steam for every kind of challenge and task—the kid who cleans off the tables with gusto, asks for the hardest book to read, and attempts the most ambitious collage. Some children, however, are motivated only for certain things: they give their all on the soccer field but seem virtually paralyzed during the academic part of the day. Or a child might dive into anything related to books and writing, but become constrained and cautious when doing math. Then there are the kids who don't seem motivated for anything. They don't try at math or reading. They don't raise their hands during group discussions. They never volunteer for special tasks. They never hustle. And yet, if you asked most teachers to line up their students from most motivated to least, they wouldn't be able to do it. Part of the reason is because children are so uneven in this regard, highly motivated for one thing but not for another. But that's not the only reason it's hard to compare children when it comes to motivation. The other reason is that, although motivation is in some ways a drive, like appetite, it is an extremely complex drive, shaped by several forces.

Scientists have learned that motivation is as much a thought process as it is a feeling. What a child *believes* about trying hard matters as much as how much get-up-and-go he has or how much he wants to do well. Carol Dweck's research (Yaeger and Dweck 2012), in particular, has shown that only some children think that effort pays off and that success is the product of industry. They tend to value small improvements as much as they do the final outcome or their standing in relation to others. They compare where they are with where they've been. They are motivated toward mastery. In contrast, some kids, who may be equally motivated, have a different goal: they are oriented toward success. They care less about getting better than they do about looking good. For these kids, a grade or a prize matters more than improvement. Studies have shown that these two orientations have significant implications for children's approach to schoolwork. For instance, in the classic demonstration, children who seek mastery will choose a harder task, knowing that though they may not succeed, it will push them to get better. Children who seek success, on the other hand, tend to choose an easier task, drawn to the prospect of winning, whatever winning might mean in a given setting. These differences in motivation seem to rest on two very different ideas about accomplishments. Children who seek mastery tend to believe that people get better at things a little at a time; progress is, in their minds, incremental. Children who seek success, on the other hand, have an implicit belief that a person is either good at something or not. What's the point in trying, if you know you have no basic talent in that endeavor?

> Scientists have learned that motivation is as much a thought process as it is a feeling.

As Ms. Endicott thought over Aida's behavior, she realized that Aida probably had an *entity* theory of ability. She thought she wasn't good at math or reading and didn't think anything could change that. It's not that she wasn't eager to do well; it's just that she hadn't acquired a belief in the power of effort and incremental progress. But such an orientation is not fixed for life. Dweck and her colleagues tried encouraging children in very specific ways. They highlighted small improvements in students' work ("You got five more problems correct today than you did last time I gave a math quiz."). They also tried explicitly teaching students that perseverance and practice lead to greater accomplishments than mere native ability. When they used these techniques, children were surprisingly quick to shift their theory of ability. And as a result, their response to academic challenges shifted as well. But what leads a child to favor one of these beliefs over another? Why did Aida have an entity theory of ability?

Needless to say, the answer is not completely straightforward. Several factors shape the amount and kind of motivation a child possesses. For instance, it's unsurprising that parents have a hand in determining their children's motivation. But the way in which they influence their children is unexpected. Researchers used to think that parents who emphasized talent would have children who carried around an entity theory. The parent who constantly said, "Well, you're just naturally good at that, so of course you won," was likely to have a child who felt there was no point in trying. By the same token, children whose parents emphasized effort by saying things like, "You may win the race this time. You practiced all summer, and that's going to make a huge difference," would be likely to have an *incremental* theory and would work hard, taking pleasure in small gains. Researchers thought, at first, that parents' own views on ability and effort would mold their children's views.

However, when Dweck and her colleagues asked subjects a series of questions about their parents' attitudes toward effort and accomplishment, young children seemed vague. It seemed they didn't have good antennae for their parents' theories of ability. However, when probed about how their parents responded to setbacks, they gave clear, definite answers. A six-year-old might not know if his mom thought it was a good thing to work at something a little every day. But he sure knew what she said and did when she was disappointed or frustrated with an outcome. He couldn't remember whether she mentioned how long he spent on his spelling words or whether his dad talked about people's natural talents. But he could tell you what his mom did when she got fired. It may well be that parents don't make many explicit comments, one way or another, about the value of persistence and effort. But in this case, actions speak louder than words. When a child hears his mother announce she finished in the slowest group during the 5K race, he may not pay much attention. But when he hears her make plans, "Starting this week, I'm going to work out five days instead of three. I want to do better next year," it sinks in. Parents' responses to their own failures make a big impression on children. Perhaps Aida's parents had kept their setbacks to themselves, or perhaps they responded to failure with sadness and alarm rather than new determination. Perhaps when Aida had hit a snag on the playground, or in kindergarten, she hadn't been encouraged to try again. But really, how would it help Ms. Endicott to speculate endlessly about Aida's home life? And thinking back to the paraprofessional, she reminded herself that it wasn't necessarily useful to think about Aida in terms of strengths and weaknesses. Could she describe her without evaluating her?

After about three weeks of writing short descriptions of Aida, taken at odd moments throughout the day, Ms. Endicott sat down and looked them over. She thought she saw a pattern blinking out at her. She consulted some articles that helped her make sense of her notes. All the times when Aida seemed to have slumped were just after the children were asked to learn a new skill or task and just before they began working on it. Challenges made Aida fade.

Ms. Endicott thought she might try encouraging Aida's small efforts, commenting more on progress and less on whether Aida's work was good or not so good, and that she could model positive responses to setbacks. In fact, she would highlight those, showing all the children that she didn't care one whit whether they succeeded at any given task, but only about their response when something was difficult. She knew, from all of her failed New Year's resolutions, that deciding to emphasize effort wasn't enough. She needed a concrete plan. She decided to keep two little lists side by side for one month. On a small pad she drew two columns. In one column she'd record, with a little check mark, every time she commented on a child's small progress or effort (she decided not to make a distinction between the things she said privately to one child and the things she said to several children or the class; she simply wanted to track her overall behavior, assuming it would eventually have a general effect). In the second column she'd note down every time she said something like, "Pete, you're so great at math." She figured she should get a clearer sense of whether she was cancelling out her efforts to foster an incremental theory of ability and performance motivation with spontaneous bursts of enthusiasm for talent and success.

Meanwhile, Ms. Endicott noticed something else that brought her up short. Looking over the various descriptions she had written, she confirmed her earlier vague impression that Aida wasn't sad all the time. Not at all. The notes made it clear that Aida came alive when she was talking with friends. She seemed energized, wittier, more verbal, and quicker to come up with astute observations. Strange as it sounded to her own ears, when Aida was with others, she seemed to brim with energy and focus. She seemed motivated.

There's almost no way to get a baby to try harder. When one is motivated, he is unstoppable (imagine a baby who is learning to walk, trying again and again, no matter how often he falls). And when he isn't interested, nothing will work (imagine getting a baby to pay attention to a movie when he's hungry). This has to do with the fact that early on, a child's immediate needs (to walk, to explore interesting new objects and events, to eat) are everything. A baby cannot imagine the future, and he cannot think abstractly, so he cannot organize his current behavior for some vague or future goal. But by the time children are six or seven, they have attained several cognitive skills that allow them to do slightly unappealing things for the sake of an appealing future goal—they can practice doing addition problems, dribbling a basketball, or playing a melody so that they will ace the test, win the game, or shine in the concert. But that works only if the test, game, or concert is in two weeks. Asking children to work hard day after day on activities at which they don't excel so that ten years later they can get into a good college is completely different. It's a strategy that is almost always doomed to fail. As Ms. Endicott thought about this, she realized that asking Aida to try harder so that she'd get better grades later wasn't going to work. But couldn't she entice Aida, bit by bit, to try harder with more short-term rewards?

Most teachers know that if they reinforce children's good behavior, with even the smallest rewards, and consistently do not reinforce bad behavior, they can shape many aspects of a child's performance. By smiling or putting a gold star next to their name each time they raise their hand to speak, and ignoring them each time they simply call out, you can condition most kids to behave in certain ways. A system of rewards and punishments, based on a behaviorist model, works quite well at helping teachers mold certain aspects of what children do in school. A gold-star plan might get results. But what *kind* of results? Ms. Endicott didn't just want Aida to comply and act like a better student. She wanted Aida to feel differently about learning.

A gold star plan might get results. But what kind of results? Ms. Endicott didn't just want Aida to comply and act like a better student. She wanted Aida to feel differently about learning.

In a classic study of motivation, psychologists Lepper and Greene (1978) invited elementary school children to join them in a small room down the hall from their regular classroom. They invited children to draw using some nice crayons and colored pens. In one condition the children were promised a small gift if they engaged in the drawing. In another condition they were not (at the end of the activity, some of these children were offered a reward anyway, while others were not). The researchers watched all of these children as they drew (the process of drawing) and analyzed the drawings themselves (the product), and then, a few days later, they once again made the drawing materials available to all the participants (another way of measuring the children's response to the original activity).

What they learned might surprise some teachers. Children who had been promised a reward seemed less engaged in the activity, drew less complex and interesting drawings (as judged by a team of trained coders), and were less interested in drawing when the materials were once again available. In other words, by adding an extrinsic reward, the researchers had lowered the intrinsic appeal of drawing. The lesson from this is pretty clear: given activities that are naturally appealing to many children (like making things), rewards hurt rather than help the learning process. Why would this be the case? Because children do what adults do—they try to make sense of the situation. Given a promise of a prize, their unconscious calculation is that the activity must be slightly dull or unpleasant if they need a prize to do it. Over time, activities that a child might have liked and been eager to work at become chores whose only appeal is the reward they might get at the end. And though the promise of a reward might work from time to time, when there is no longer a reward attached to the activity, the child is likely to abandon the topic as quickly as she can. If you doubt this, just think of the books you might have loved reading, if they hadn't been assigned at school. What did Aida find absorbing?

Ms. Endicott made an inventory of the activities in which Aida seemed alive, interested, attentive, and activated, and the activities in which she seemed to withdraw or turn down her psychological volume. Sure enough, Aida was most alive when she was talking or working with friends, least alive when she was isolated from friends. The one writing activity that she perked up for was when she and a few friends were allowed to write a play instead of a story or a report. She particularly enjoyed writing the dialogue and describing the personalities of each character. Being with her friends was the surest way to energize Aida. But there were small hints that her interest in people extended beyond the immediate. Yes, she liked lunch period and hallway chatter. But there was more to Aida than that. When Ms. Endicott looked over her notes again, she saw that Aida had leaned in eagerly the day they discussed a book about a little boy who felt like an outsider in his town. If ever a child had embodied engagement, it was Aida listening to that story. She had also seemed unusually animated and interested when the class had worked together on a big class poster about how to handle conflict. All along Ms. Endicott had assumed that Aida's social liveliness was, at the least, irrelevant to her academic success and more likely an impediment to her learning. But what if she turned that around? What if she thought about Aida's time with friends as a clue to her interests?

Ms. Endicott began to wonder whether it made any sense to ask Aida to apply herself to tasks that isolated her from other kids and that seemed far removed from the things that mattered to her. And yet, Ms. Endicott knew that Aida had to make progress in addition, place value, and spelling. There was so much she needed to master this year in order to do well going forward. Hitting just above the thirtieth percentile in math didn't seem good enough, given her potential. Thinking about this brought to mind an image of Aida sitting at one of the worktables, head bent over her paper, hair falling limp in front of her eyes. And then, out of nowhere, Ms. Endicott imagined Aida as a four-year-old, laughing and making up crazy rhymes with her friends. She had probably been a bouncy little girl, brimming with funny thoughts and games. That had been a mere three years before.

Ms. Endicott had been so focused on where Aida (and all of her second graders) needed to go that she had lost sight of where Aida had been. And yet seven-year-olds are more closely connected to their younger selves than they are to their future selves. Not long before, like all three- and four-year-olds, Aida had been powered by her own intrinsic interests, perhaps inventing scenarios with her friends, spending time planning the rules of their games, spending hours adorning themselves in the dress-up corner and enacting the roles of doctors, firemen, and mommies. She had worked hard at playing with friends and mimicking the rules and information of the adult world around her. Isn't that what all the time in the dress-up corner had given her?

Each time two friends giggle during reading time, a teacher takes that in as one more piece of evidence that friends shouldn't work together. But because of the way confirmation bias functions, they might not even notice all the times children get more out of what they read because they are reacting to it with a buddy.

As Ms. Endicott daydreamed about four-year-old Aida, it dawned on her that second grade could build on those interests and energies, rather than abruptly replace them.

As Ms. Endicott mulled over ways to use her new-found insights, something worried her. Her impulse was to make the social world more central to Aida's school day. But the conventional wisdom said that friends would distract Aida from learning. The trouble with conventional wisdom, however, is that it's often wrong. People pass on ideas to one another, and if the ideas feel right, those ideas settle in and eventually seem like facts. Once such a fact has taken hold, people tend to notice when something confirms it and overlook the experiences that don't. This is known as confirmation bias, and everyone is vulnerable to it. But for teachers, confirmation bias can play out in particular ways unique to educational settings. So, for instance, many teachers lean toward the idea that friends distract one another. Schedules are created to ensure children socialize at recess and learn during class time. The idea that friends and learning are a bad mix tends to get reinforced by daily encounters. Each time two friends giggle during reading time, a teacher takes that in as one more piece of evidence that friends shouldn't work together. But because of the way confirmation bias functions, they might not even notice all the times children get more out of what they read *because* they are reacting to it with a buddy. There's nothing wrong with confirmation bias; it's human. However, it can get in the way of good teaching practice. Luckily, in this case we have data to overrule the conventional wisdom and overpower our confirmation bias. The data show that kids actually get more out of their academic tasks when they can work with the friends they choose. Though there are risks (giggling, chatting, distraction), those risks are far outweighed by the benefits, which include enjoyment, a sense of well-being, a feeling of autonomy and choice, and opportunities for collaboration. This last one is particularly interesting because it is counterintuitive. The prohibition against cheating, or leaning on others' learning rather than on one's own, can obscure a fundamental truth about learning: learning is almost always a collaborative process. Most teachers put kids into work groups some of the time, but they might make collaboration more central if they understood how powerfully it supports intellectual growth.

Aida found time with her friends to be meaningful. But there was more to it than that. She had also brought her seven-year-old mind to the topic of friendships. She liked being with friends but also thinking about friends. This explained why she was so interested in sorting out social conflicts and mulling over moral dilemmas in reading time and social studies projects. Her energy for friends had begun to shape her intellectual concerns. Ms. Endicott could use that.

She decided that she would invite Aida and her friends to form a work club. Each day the work club would get forty-five minutes to school one another on the things they found hardest to do. Each child in the club would have a chance to teach the others at whichever skill he or she excelled. Ms. Endicott started by getting each child in the group to identify the thing he or she felt most competent to teach. Aida chose Spanish, which she had always spoken with her grandmother. Being an expert at something, and sharing that expertise with other kids, was just one more way for her to become invested in school. Aida and her friends loved the club. After six weeks, they gave a demonstration of what they had each taught each other to all the other kids in the class (who had long since formed their own clubs).

Next, Ms. Endicott suggested to Aida and a few of her friends that they write a play together rather than write about the books they had read. They could use language arts time to plan their play and could perform it for the class in a few weeks. The girls loved the idea. But people don't change overnight. Even children. Aida sat quietly while the others argued about what the plot of the play should be. She seemed, once again, to be fading. Ms. Endicott, who had dropped by for a few minutes each morning to eavesdrop as the girls tangled over the direction of the play, saw an opening for providing a little more guidance. She said to them, "Plays need to have a problem in them. Maybe you can make a play where a group of kids fight about something and then figure out a solution." She had, quite casually, taught them something essential about good writing and good storytelling, skills that were key to her language arts curriculum. But just as importantly, she had provided them with a plot idea that she knew would draw Aida back out of her shell. Knowing a lot about what goes into good writing, and knowing a lot more than she had about Aida, provided Ms. Endicott with a suggestion worth a week of lessons. As she left the group, she heard Aida say, "Let's make the gang of friends find a llama walking down the street, and then they can fight about who gets to keep the llama."

That paraprofessional had opened a door for Ms. Endicott. She began by thinking about the nature of motivation and engagement in seven- and eight-year-olds. Then she deliberately set about to notice where and when Aida was engaged. Finally, she reconstructed the road Aida must have travelled to become a seven-year-old who felt reluctant to try hard at difficult things. Ms. Endicott found a few simple ways to help Aida try hard and to transform tedious and futile hours into something Aida could plunge into. Recess was no longer the only part of the day where Aida came alive.

CHAPTER TWO

Do Children Learn to Think in School?

———— ◆ ————

Cognition: Part One ⋆ Skill Acquisition ⋆
Major Theories of Development

LOUISE STOOD IN the doorway and took stock of her classroom. The desks were pushed together in clusters of four, and though none of her students was there at the moment, she could envision each group of nine- and ten-year-olds who sat together. As she did every year within the first week of school, she had placed kids together according to her own somewhat quirky internal rubric—two shy kids who needed to be with more gregarious ones, very bright kids who, she felt sure, needed to be with other whizzes, and a student with a diagnosis of high-functioning autism who needed to be with a few children who could handle his quirks. She looked over at the shelves that divided the desks from the open area where she held meetings. She loved her shelves. On the side facing the desks were all kinds of inviting materials: an unusual collection of pens and pencils; all kinds of lined paper for writing as well as paper of different colors and textures for collage; scissors; glue; three baskets of interesting materials—felt scraps, ribbons and string, small stones she had collected over the years whenever she was by the water; and a large jar containing about four hundred buttons of every style, which she had bought at a tag sale.

On the opposite side of the barrier, the shelves contained books. Many, many books, of all kinds. She knew that to encourage her fourth graders to read, she had to offer them lots of options—mysteries, nonfiction, and funny poems, as well as some of the classics, like the Red Wall series, *Hatchet*, and the *Chronicles of Narnia*. Over in the far corner of the room she had set up a science counter. It contained three microscopes, a scale, and several trays containing the equipment needed for the experiments she periodically guided the children through—tweezers, droppers, tongue depressors, and glass slides. Then her eyes travelled across the back wall to the opposite corner. That's where she stored the textbooks and workbooks: a set of fourth-grade readers designed to follow the Common Core, a set of the math workbooks the faculty had chosen together, the Interactive Science texts, and workbooks, and finally her social studies collection. Her eyes shifted upward, as she looked over the posters on the wall. She had one that listed the class' common rules of conduct—the kids had written them, and reading them over made her feel good: "There is no I in Team," "Ask Three Before Me," "There are no stupid questions," "Look over your work," "Try your hardest," and "NO BULLYING." Each rule had been written by a different team of kids, and was brightly colored with lively little illustrations next to it. The adjacent wall was covered in whiteboard. On the upper left-hand corner she had written out the schedule. She changed various elements now and then, but for the most part it remained pretty much the same from September to June.

8:35 a.m.–8:40 a.m.—Meet and Greet

8:45 a.m.–9:30 a.m.—Math

9:35 a.m.–10:10 a.m.—Reading

10:10 a.m.–10:20 a.m.—Snack and Recess

10:25 a.m.–11:05 a.m.—Language Arts Work Groups

11:10 a.m.–11:45 a.m.—Art/Music

11:50 a.m.–12:15 p.m.—Lunch and Recess

12:20 p.m.–1:00 p.m.—Quiet Reading

1:05 p.m.–1:40 p.m.—Social Studies

1:45 p.m.–2:25 p.m.—Science/Projects

Louise wondered for a moment if it was too crammed. As she looked it over, she could hear the bell ringing at the end of every period and see, in her mind's eye, her students pushing back their chairs and shuffling and jouncing their way from one activity to the next. The times they had to line up, or put one book away to get out another, seemed like punctuation marks that came too frequently, before the sentences were really finished. As she mentally replayed a typical day, these frequent transitions struck her as abrupt and intrusive. But what could she omit? The subjects were mandatory, and she tried to let the kids do hands-on activities as much as possible. They used stuff from her delicious shelves of materials for book reports, science projects, and social studies posters. She felt she did a pretty good job of spicing up the fairly relentless pace of the day. And with that, Louise shook off her reverie. Time to give the students some written feedback, before they arrived, in twenty minutes.

She settled into her chair and began going through a stack of paragraphs the children had written about the books they were reading. Though commenting was tedious, it gave her a chance to make sure her kids were making progress. These short essays were pretty good! Of the twenty-two kids, sixteen seemed to have learned how to start with a topic sentence. The punctuation was fairly accurate in most of them, and she found only eight or nine examples of incomplete sentences, all from just three kids she knew were struggling. That was a big improvement over the beginning of the year, when most of them seemed so casual about what was and wasn't a sentence. Her brief practice sessions, in which she asked them to circle incomplete sentences, must have paid off. She wasn't so sure about their vocabulary though. The weekly vocabulary quizzes were getting harder, as planned, and the kids seemed to be keeping pace with them. The average score was 84 percent; that seemed fine to her. But when she read over their own writing, she noticed that very few were actually using new or unusual words.

Louise's thoughts moved on to math. She had made a grid to keep track of her students' progress. On the left she made a column where she listed each child's name. Across the top she made a row listing the sixteen skills and competencies the fourth-grade team had decided were the most important ones, pulled together from their textbook and the Common Core. It included items like *Understands inverse operations* and *Solves problems with line plots*. She used the weekly quizzes as guides for checking off when she felt that a child had mastered one of the skills. Her goal was that there would be at least twelve of the items checked off by June. She was determined to keep the kids moving through the textbook. And she enjoyed finding ways to make each new concept or skill engaging to them. She spent time thinking of great real-life examples: how you would divide up a bowl of chili for people with different appetites, different ways to measure the distance between the school building and each child's home, and little gambling games to teach them the basics of probability. She knew how to keep the pace going, so they'd do fifteen minutes of a fun hands-on activity and then fifteen minutes of practicing a skill using its matching worksheet.

She took a sip of her tea. She could hear the buses arriving, and she knew her classroom was about to erupt with the sounds and smells of twenty-two nine- and ten-year-olds. The first one in was Luis. He was one of her brightest students—the one who lit up the day, even when everything else was going wrong. He was cheerful and popular, fun for other kids, and yet very focused on his work. He liked her, but he was no teacher's pet. He was just a really great kid. He bounded over to her desk and said, "Hi, Ms. Cuthbert. Robotics this afternoon, right? I'm psyched." She had been so focused on taking stock of the kids' progress, she had forgotten that today was her long day at school.

The summer before, Louise had taken a three-week workshop on robotics. She couldn't believe how much she loved it. In fact, she thought, "In another life I might have gone into computer science or engineering." So in September when the principal had asked teachers to offer six-week after-school programs for a small stipend, she had decided to lead one for building robots. Nine kids had signed up. And when the six weeks were over, the kids begged her to do it for another six weeks. Here they were in March, and they were into their third round. All nine kids had stuck with it, and two more had joined. They were now way beyond what she had learned during her summer workshop. It was funny, she thought. It had never occurred to her to measure what they were learning in robotics club. Now that she thought about it, she realized she didn't need to measure it. They were learning by leaps and bounds. She glanced over at the shelf that was high above the science counter. That was where she kept the robots they were in the midst of building. When she thought back to the ones they had made in October, it was so obvious that they had progressed to a whole new level of complexity and skill. "Hmm," she thought. "Funny to think that I have to work so hard to get math concepts across to them, but the robotics seem to teach themselves." Then the bell rang and it was time to begin the day.

A few weeks later, Louise was at a family reunion. Her cousin Cora was there. Cora worked on a design team for a small company that designed a wide range of cool objects—bags, socks, and other gift items. At forty-three, she was one of the more senior people at the company, which often hired people right out of college. During dinner, Cora began to talk about some of the new designers they had just hired. "A few of them are just terrific. They come up with great ideas, they figure out how to implement them, and they know how to explain it to others. But jeez. Not many. More are like, 'Uh, what did you want me to do?' I mean, they're great once you give them an instruction. They know their stuff. They're smart. But they don't seem to come up with anything on their own. They don't know how to take a suggestion and run with it. They are always waiting to carry out someone else's plan. And then you've got the other ones, just as bad. You know, the ones who spin these great ideas and you're like, 'OK, awesome. Go with it.' But they have no follow-through. They aren't able to think through what it would take to make their idea happen. It seems like the kids we hire are smart and they've gone to good schools. But I'm not sure they know how to think." She turned to Louise. "You're the teacher in the family. When do kids start learning how to think?"

Cora's question stopped Louise in her tracks. She realized that everyone assumes that school helps children learn to think. But could she answer Cora's question? Did she know when children started thinking? Did she even have a clear sense of whether it was something children actually learned, like multiplication or basketball, or whether it was something that simply matured, like teeth or walking? More perplexing even than that, *was* she actually helping them become better thinkers and, if so, in what way? To answer that, she'd have to go back to the beginning. When do children begin thinking?

The Dawn of Thinking

Children begin making sense of the world from the moment they are born. On her first day out of the womb, a baby responds differently to a familiar voice (her mother's) than an unfamiliar one (a nurse's, for instance). She begins separating the world into experiences she has encountered before (her father bending down to lift her out of her bassinet) and ones she hasn't (someone new coming within her view). She doesn't just *notice* when something is new. She pays more attention to it. When researchers show babies a series of screen images of, say, teddy bears, they look at each image. But when, on the sixth round, the research projects a screen image of, say, a car, the babies notice that they are encountering something new and different. When that happens, their heart rate changes, they produce more moisture on their skin, their breathing changes, and they look longer. Once they've noticed that something is different, they study the new image in order to make it familiar. We even know when it has become familiar and when they feel ready to move on. Humans come wired to try to make sense of whatever they don't already know and to make the unfamiliar familiar. This ability underlies our enormous capacity to take in information, which is key to thinking.

Babies' nearly ravenous appetite for paying attention to new things, and studying them until those new things are familiar, explains why they are such outstanding learners, in some ways at the height of their learning capacity. After all, by age three, nearly all children have learned to talk, they know the basic routines of everyday life, and they have become capable of grouping things into conceptual categories (what happens at breakfast; farm animals; shoes). These skills (language, routines, and concepts) form the foundation of most later intellectual work. But that's not all they've learned by the age of three. They are also quite adept at navigating the social world (how to get a cookie from Grandpa, what to do when another child wants the same toy, and what to do when Mom is mad). Children become quite skilled at everyday tasks that require good thinking—they can set the table for the right number of people (one father, one sister, one cousin, and oneself: four plates), they can figure out how to make a stepstool out of boxes to climb up and reach an interesting object on the counter, and they know how to ask the right question to get the information they seek. When you think about it, during those first four years of life, without any formal instruction, children acquire more information and new (and important) skills than they ever will again. How do young children accomplish all this impressive learning and thinking?

Children Think with Their Bodies and Their Words

At first children learn, and learn to think, by poking, banging, lifting, stacking, and climbing (not to mention tasting, whacking, pinching, and smelling). In other words, they use their mouths, their hands, and their feet to test and revise their theories about the world. Through their actions they explore the unknown and make sense of the unfamiliar. Jean Piaget's research showed that there is a scientist in every child (Gopnik, Meltzoff, and Kuhl 1999). Just as importantly, he showed that in the first few years of life, children do their thinking with their bodies. An eighteen-month-old doesn't sit quietly in a chair, watching events unfold and listening to others talk, as she contemplates an explanation for what she sees. But every time she *does* something—puts a small toy in her mouth or pulls a plug out of the wall—she is testing her expectations about how things work and revising those expectations based on what happens. In a remarkably short period of time, by the age of three or four, children know how to generate hypotheses and test those hypotheses: whether a particular object will float or not, how high you can stack blocks before they will topple over, and what will happen if you throw something at your brother. This capacity is not the result of particularly skilled or thoughtful parenting. Children in all settings construct ideas about the world around them and then test to see if their ideas hold up. But they need to act in order to test their ideas. In fact, recent research shows that when children hand print or write letters, as opposed to typing them, they learn more about phonics. The research suggests that the part of the brain involved with motor activity is linked to the part of the brain that is learning the meaning of those letters. To stifle the body is to limit the mind.

By three, most children have also begun to ask questions, which exponentially expands the possibilities of what they can learn about. They ask what, when, and where questions (for instance, "What's that called?" "Where's the cat?" and "When can I have ice cream?"). But they also ask why and how questions ("Why is the ice melting?" "How do people get to the top?" and "Why did Grandpa die?"). How and why questions allow them to seek explanations. They can now inquire about things they cannot directly test through poking, lifting, and manipulating the world around them. Two- and three-year-olds ask, on average, about 27 questions per hour, and some ask as many as 104 per hour. Clearly they have tremendous energy for trying to understand the complex world of which they are a part. Some of their questions are about the physical world. They want to know about how the duck swims, what makes ice melt, and why the door bangs. But not all of their questions are about the immediate world around them. Some of their questions are about the meanings of words, what makes something fair, and why some friends have two parents and others just one. In other words, they become interested in concepts and phenomena beyond the immediate world around them. They begin to explore and create ideas. But psychologists haven't always known that.

In the early part of the twentieth century, the work of Jean Piaget (1967) and other developmental psychologists like Lev Vygotsky (1980) had us pretty well convinced that before the age of about eleven, children were not capable of such abstract thought. Research at that time suggested that very young children could think only about things they could see and hear right around them. Though in some ways those researchers were correct, their insights were constrained by the experimental methods available to them, which led them to a somewhat distorted view of children. Take, for example, Piaget's well-known claim that very young children are limited by their egocentrism, unable to think about how the world looks from any perspective but their own. He demonstrated this egocentrism with his famous three-mountain task (Piaget and Inhelder 1969). Children sat at a table facing a 3-D diorama of mountains of different heights. On the other side of the table was a doll. From his or her seat, the child could see a small figure (for instance, a fox) on the side of one of the mountains. But the fox was placed in such a way that a person (or in this case, doll) sitting opposite from the child would not be able to see it. When Piaget asked three- and four-year-olds whether the doll could also see the fox, children said yes, certain that the doll could see whatever the children saw. Piaget took this to mean that children could not envision what things looked like from anyone's perspective but their own. The method was brilliant in that it showed scientists that you could figure out what was going on inside children's minds by devising scenarios that made their thoughts visible. But in the three-mountain task, at least, his particular conclusion was only partly correct.

A British researcher named Margaret Donaldson (1979) suspected that children might be able to imagine the perspective of someone else, and might want to, if the problem they were asked was more engaging and meaningful to them. To test her hunch, she showed children a large square divided by two walls, so that there were four quadrants. She told each young subject that a child named Tommy had stolen a cookie and that now two policemen were looking for him. Tommy, she explained, wanted to hide from the policemen, who were stationed at two positions around the perimeter of the diagram. Then Donaldson asked each child, "Where should Tommy hide so that the police can't find him?" Given this very engaging and plausible story, where perspective taking was required to help Tommy hide effectively, children were quite adept. The majority could locate the one quadrant not visible to either policeman, even though from their own vantage point they could still see Tommy.

Presented with a situation in which imagining someone else's point of view would help solve a problem that interested them, children used more advanced cognition than Piaget and others thought possible. In the years since those experiments researchers have continued to uncover a formidable array of thinking skills that even very young children demonstrate. For instance, Karen Wynn (1998) and her colleagues have shown that even six-month-olds react with surprise when they watch a toy duck placed next to another, then a screen drops down for just a second, and when it lifts back up, there are not two but three ducks. Showing that one plus one adds up to three surprises them. Wynn's experiments suggest that perhaps even infants have a rudimentary grasp of arithmetic.

As Louise delved into the literature on how children acquire thinking skills, she realized that while teachers were focused on *what* children knew, researchers had been looking at something slightly different. They were interested in *how* young children made sense of the world and asking whether that basic sense-making changed as children got older. A teacher might notice whether his students could identify common phonetic combinations in words, hear syllables, tell time, or show some fundamental sense of fractions. But researchers, meanwhile, were asking whether children first categorized the material world in terms of function (all the things Mom used in the garden) or form (all round things) and what led them to more abstract ways of forming concepts.

Louise also realized that scientists had been revising their ideas about what children could do, intellectually, at what age. But one thing seemed to have stood the test of time. Children don't simply get better at thinking bit by bit, one piece of information or new skill at a time. Piaget had been right about that all along. The way children mentally experience the world goes through a series of sea changes, and these sea changes occur in an orderly way. No typically developing child is born thinking about abstract properties of say, number, and then later begins holding and banging things as a way of learning about them. In other words, the most important shifts in the way children think unfold in a sequence. Though one child may go through the sequence more quickly than another, the order doesn't change. More importantly, those changes aren't simply an increase in specific skills. The world looks and feels different to a four-year-old than it does to a seven-year-old. Louise began to zero in on her own classroom. How did the world look to nine-year-olds? How did they put together their thoughts?

You can show formal algebra problems to a seven-year-old until you are blue in the face, but all she will see is a string of numbers and symbols that mean little to her. Someone might be able to train a seven-year-old to follow a set of procedures that makes it seem like she understands algebra, but until she can think about the ways in which symbols represent abstract properties of the world, and the invisible rules that explain all manner of natural phenomena, she won't actually understand. She'll be *performing* math but not *thinking* math.

Which is not to say she isn't thinking about the kinds of problems that underlie algebra. For instance, without even realizing it, a child of six or seven will encounter the fact that order matters for some things and not for others. Whether a child begins with four pieces of candy and then adds two or begins with two and adds four, she will end up with six. But if she's building a fortress, she will discover that she can't put the roof on until she's made the walls.

What does this mean to a teacher? It means that you don't need to "make children think." They come to school already having devoted enormous resources and time to thinking. And all along they have been revising their thoughts to take into account new experiences. Thus even without a teacher, nearly all children become capable of thinking in increasingly powerful ways. But it also means that every time a teacher decides to teach a certain intellectual skill, he or she should think carefully about two important things: how the skill builds on what the child already knows or thinks and how the student sees the world. What an apple, a division sign, a word problem, or a story about the past means to an adult says little about what it means to children who are five, seven, or nine years old. Thinking and doing academic work are not the same things.

The Expanding Repertoire of Mental Tools

Piaget and those who followed him focused on figuring out the stages by which children became capable of higher-order thinking. But not everyone thought that was the right way to characterize the growth of children's minds. The great American developmental psychologist Jerome Bruner (1966) argued that Piaget's view was too linear. He showed that instead of leaving each way of thinking behind as children acquired more powerful intellectual structures, children hold on to old ways of thinking. By the time children are in school they use three systems to understand the world: they act on it (touch, open, build), they represent it for themselves through pretend play, pictures, buildings, action, and imagery, and they use symbols (at first with labels and names, then with stories and explanations, and finally with mathematical equations and arguments). But he saw no evidence that children leave behind action for imagery, and imagery for symbols. Instead, he claimed, the sophisticated symbol user (the high school student, for instance) still uses action and imagery to understand the world and think about things, and if adults create the right opportunities, children will elaborate each of these three ways of knowing so that they are ever more powerful and give children access to ever more complex realms of thought. Contemporary psychologists like Robert Siegler (1998) have shown that as children get older their repertoire expands, and their ability to choose the right strategy for a given situation improves. He gives the following wonderful example: If you ask a five-year-old what five plus two is, he is likely to count on his fingers. But an eight-year-old may well give you an answer from rote memory. However, by eight, and then beyond, there are some situations when counting on your fingers is still a pretty effective strategy. Development, in this view, is less about discarding old ways of thinking for better ones, and more about broadening the range of strategies children can draw upon, as well as their ability to choose the right one under any given circumstance. Within this framework, the focus in school should be less on getting children to give up immature ways of thinking for more sophisticated methods and more on helping them expand their repertoire and choose an approach that fits a situation. Even in adulthood there might be times when counting fingers or apples is better than scribbling on a page or doing mental calculations. So too, even in adulthood there are times when the story is more important to think about than the choice of words or the identification of tropes in a piece of writing.

Louise just couldn't get enough of this idea. What if she focused on helping her students collect intellectual strategies, instead of showing them how to do things the "fourth-grade way"? Take Luis and the other kids in the robotics program. During math time, she made sure they weren't counting on their fingers, were learning to borrow and carry, and were using basic operations to solve word problems. The book took them from one way of working with numbers to another way. But in robotics they seemed to go back and forth between building their machines through trial and error and thinking through a plan before they made it. What was wrong with blending those two strategies? She began to think that when she herded them toward a specified procedure or method, they got better at it but didn't understand much. When they worked on problems they cared about, and had the freedom to mess around and pick and choose their own solutions, they got just as far and seemed to understand much more. But Louise knew that simply leaving them to play with machine parts wasn't enough. She knew she had a role to play.

Children Do Not Develop on Their Own

Piaget had assumed that children everywhere were alike. All they had to do was have opportunities to interact with the world around them (whatever the particulars of their world contained) and they'd end up arriving at the same place (abstract thinking). But Lev Vygotsky, the brilliant young psychologist who worked before and after the Russian Revolution, argued that Piaget's view had overlooked the importance of other people. His work showed that development was not a solitary process. Children don't learn to think only by interacting with objects around them (pebbles, blocks, twigs, Legos, stacking cups, empty gourds, etc.). They learn to think, in great part, because of how others around them think and do things. Imagine, for instance, a little girl living in an apartment in Detroit. Her mother works in a car factory, and her father is a nurse. Both parents read a lot and use technology easily. Now imagine that there is a basket of objects that tumbles over onto the floor and the little girl and her father begin to sort the stuff from the basket so that they can put it into smaller baskets. Perhaps the little girl puts all the things she likes into one basket and all the things her parents like into another basket. As she puts a small stuffed bear into the basket with her favorite spoon, he might say to her, "Here, why don't I put the spoon with the other kitchen utensils, and then you can put all the toys in a separate box?" But now imagine the same child, growing up in a place where reading and technology are not important, where instead, everyday tasks are the most important thing. There, not only would the items in the spilled basket be different, but more importantly, the help of the dad would be quite different. In this scenario, the dad might say instead, "Here, why don't we put all the things for outside work in one pile and all the things for inside work in another?"

Vygotsky, and those who later built on his early discoveries, showed that children's thinking is shaped not only by their direct encounters with the world but equally by the help and suggestions they get from others in their community. In this way, a child's thinking is shaped as much by the ideas and cognitive solutions of her culture as she is by her own actions. This means, among other things, that thinking is, from the start, a social process and reflects the particular habits and priorities of one's community. As Louise read this material, something clicked. She realized that she played a totally different role in the robotics group. In her regular classes she led students in activities designed to provide them with information and new skills. Sometimes she taught them new information and procedures they didn't yet know. But when she was working with her students in the robotics club, her role seemed more informal. She didn't have enough information to deliver anything. And because it was outside of the standard curriculum, she felt no rush to impart certain skills. And yet, she found herself pointing out similarities between past problems and solutions and whatever current obstacle or challenge the children faced while making their machines. She often simply put their gestures into words: "It looks like this time those little parts aren't strong enough to hold the metal grasper at the end of the arm. What did you do last time to strengthen the extension of the machine?" She suggested; she observed; she articulated. But she didn't really instruct. She thought to herself, "This is why they seem to be learning more in robotics. You can't instruct someone to think. You can help them as they engage in new ways of thinking."

For a teacher like Louise, the volume of scientific literature on children's thinking was somewhat overwhelming. There was so much to keep track of and so many kinds of research to integrate. In order to figure out whether her classroom was helping kids learn to think, what she needed was a concise summary of the most important ideas.

A Quick Sketch of Intellectual Development

Children begin making sense of the world at birth, quickly noticing patterns and routines. Those patterns and routines are the building blocks of their early thought, allowing them to develop basic scripts for how the world works, seek regularities, and notice anything new or surprising. That cycle enables them to build up a complex store of information and keep an eye out for all new information. In the first year of life they gather information and solve problems through their actions (they watch, they grab, they listen, they bite, they pat, they stack, they kick, they climb). By two, they can represent the world (they do this every time they use a fork as an airplane or a hairbrush as a pretend telephone, pretend to drink tea, be a monster, a mommy, or superman). Then they learn to talk. At first they name the world around them, but soon enough they begin talking about it; they can ask questions, describe alternative scenarios, speculate, and plan. In some ways that shift is the most important intellectual shift of all. Because once they can use language that way, the world of problems and solutions expands exponentially.

When children are three, four, and five, the world around them presents plenty of interesting problems to them: how to reach a cookie on the counter, how to convince your father to let you have ice cream in the morning, what bugs do when you create a wall of sugar cubes, what's inside a rotten pumpkin, how to get back the truck the other child has taken from you, why some foods stay in the freezer and others sit on the shelf, and what happens to a pile of dirt when you keep adding water to it. It also offers all kinds of potential solutions: to reach the cookie they can turn a chair upside down and try to climb on it, stand on top of another child's back, or pile pillows up. To solve the problem of why some foods stay in the freezer, they can try and detect a pattern, or they can simply ask until they get a satisfying answer. There are solutions for helping them do things and explanations for helping them understand things (some of the time they can work out their own explanations, whether correct or not, and some of the time they need to solicit them from a more knowledgeable person). To young children, the world is buzzing with problems and they are perfectly equipped and quite driven to solve those problems in all kinds of ways. They are apprentices in human problem solving.

As Louise mapped what she now knew about intellectual development onto the activities in her classroom, she stumbled on a glaring mismatch she had never before considered. She could think of all kinds of things kids had to do in school that seemed totally unlike the kinds of thinking children did anywhere else.

Learning to Do School

By the time children are in first grade, we expect them to have become adept at a whole slew of skills that are unique to school. They need to raise their hand if they want to use the bathroom, stand in line to get lunch, solve problems that don't actually need to be solved, and learn all kinds of new rituals and conventions. Depending on their lives at home, things like math problems, sharing space and objects with others, and following detailed instructions might be new as well. Margaret Donaldson (1979) tells the following anecdote to illustrate this shift. A little girl comes home from her first day of school and when her mother asks her how it was, her mouth turns down in disappointment and her eyes show sad confusion. "It wasn't good. I never got the present." The mother says, "What present? What are you talking about?" And the little girl says, "When I got there, the teacher asked me my name, and I told her, and she pointed to a chair and said, 'Why don't you sit there for the present.' But she never gave me the present." Because the little girl didn't yet know the phrases and conventions of life at school, she spent a good bit of the day mystified. An even more whimsical version of this comes to life in Astrid Lindgren's classic children's book *Pippi Longstocking* (1950). Pippi, with her bright red braids and her powerful limbs, has lived a unique life, growing up without parents but with plenty of adventure and excitement. In most ways she is far more capable and independent than other children her age. And yet, she's never been to school. So when the more conventional children Tommy and Annika, who live down the road, convince her to come to school with them, she's in for some surprises.

[The teacher says to Pippi,] "Suppose we test you a little and see what you know. You are a big girl and no doubt know a great deal already. Let us begin with arithmetic. Pippi, can you tell me what seven and five are?"

Pippi, astonished and dismayed, looked at her and said, "Well, if you don't know that yourself, you needn't think I'm going to tell you."

All the children stared in horror at Pippi, and the teacher explained that one couldn't answer that way in school.

"I beg your pardon," said Pippi contritely. "I didn't know that. I won't do it again."

"No, let us hope not," said the teacher. "And now I will tell you that seven and five are twelve."

> "See that!" said Pippi. "You knew it yourself. Why are you asking then?" . . .
>
> [A little later the teacher says,] "Can Tommy answer this one?" "If Lisa has seven apples and Axel has nine apples, how many apples do they have together?"
>
> "Yes, you tell, Tommy," Pippi interrupted, "and tell me too, if Lisa gets a stomach-ache and Axel gets more stomach-ache, whose fault is it and where did they get hold of the apples in the first place?" (52–54)

Pippi has never learned the conventions of school behavior. Her outrageous but beguiling mistakes bring to life the formalisms of school thinking that we usually take for granted.

Research has amplified what Astrid Lindgren intuited. Inside of a classroom, children often encounter conventions and learning methods that are neither natural to them nor particularly effective. Take for instance, the research of George Miller, one of the founders of the field of cognitive psychology. Late in his life he began to investigate how children learned word meanings. At the time, in the 1980s, most children in this country were given lists of words each week and asked to look up the meanings and then use each word correctly in a sentence. Because students were looking up the meanings themselves, educators were confident that they were being active and therefore likely to get something out of the assignment. Miller was skeptical that children would benefit from learning meanings separate from the sentences and paragraphs in which they encountered those words. He was sure that the actual context in which one encountered a word was essential to actually learning anything useful about the word. To test his hunch, he created the LUCAS (look up and create a sentence) task (Miller 1991). In one condition children learned the dictionary meanings of words and then were asked to use those words in a sentence. The sentences kids came up with were hilarious (for instance, "The milk was virginal" and "I agitated my cereal"). They were also usually wrong, or technically correct but useless in terms of everyday conversation or writing. Miller and his colleagues contrasted the formal school method of teaching vocabulary with a more informal approach: giving children repeated opportunities to encounter the new words in interesting books and conversation. This approach did not help them offer concise definitions. But they easily and quickly learned the meanings of the words and, just as importantly, used the new words correctly when they talked and wrote.

When children get to school, the problems they must solve are often of a whole new kind—more abstract, less related to their immediate needs and desires. Moreover,

When children get to school the problems they must solve are often of a whole new kind—more abstract, less related to their immediate needs and desires. Moreover, the solutions are judged not by whether the answers feel satisfying, or the strategy gets them what they want, but because someone tells them they have done it correctly.

the solutions are judged not by whether the answers feel satisfying, or the strategy gets them what they want, but by whether someone tells them they have done it correctly or not. There were just an awful lot of skills kids needed to master for school that might help them do well in school but not make them better thinkers. Where did all of this leave Louise?

What Kinds of Thinking Do Children Learn in School?

Louise thought she had done a really nice job of making schooly things seem fun. She encouraged the kids to illustrate their book reports and use all kinds of neat objects like colored sea glass, beads, and buttons to figure out certain kinds of math problems. She made other less concrete types of work fun too: the kids had races to do their addition and subtraction facts, had celebrations for finishing sections of their math workbooks, and made their own covers for their readers. More importantly she tried to be inventive in finding ways to help children understand work that baffled them. Trudy was a good example.

The year before, a little girl named Trudy had been completely stumped by long division. She couldn't learn the steps, no matter how many times they went over it. So Louise had brought in some jars and jelly beans. She sat down with Trudy and said, "Look, let's count the jelly beans." They counted to 112. "And how many jars are there?" Trudy quickly counted 8 jars. "If we want to put the same number into each jar, we'll be dividing 112 by 8. How many will go into each jar? Let's go jar by jar, jellybean by jellybean." Trudy happily put a bean in each of the eight jars, until she had filled each one with a bean. Then she started over. When she had no more jellybeans left, Louise asked her how many were in each jar. Trudy had been keeping track, so she knew there were 14 in each jar. Louise said, "Congratulations! You just did long division." Trudy smiled, with a somewhat bewildered look on her face. The next morning, as Louise handed Trudy her long division worksheet, she said, "This should make a little more sense to you now, eh?" Trudy took the paper with a wary look on her face. Watching Trudy's confusion, Louise realized that for Trudy, the thinking involved in dropping the jellybeans into the jars had almost nothing to do with the thinking involved in solving long division problems on paper. One was fairly intuitive and a natural extension of the way Trudy solved all kinds of problems. Dropping one jellybean at a time until they were all equally dispersed is clever and inventive—a solution many kids might naturally hit upon themselves. But translating that into a symbolic representation, or a set of rules that capture a mathematical rule, is less intuitive. Plenty of kids learn how to do such problems on paper, but that doesn't mean they have any better a grasp of it than Trudy did. For some children, without the right kind of help from a teacher, the beans in the jar don't ever morph into abstract understanding of the math. And for other kids, the math on paper is easy enough, but they have no better grasp of the underlying mathematical principles than Trudy did.

Louise began to wonder whether she was mushing up two different educational goals. One set of goals involved teaching children the right procedures for solving various kinds of academic tasks: things like the order of operations, translating word problems into number sentences, identifying the different parts of a sentence, spelling, and vocabulary. The other goal was to guide them toward identifying problems (all kinds of problems) on their own and then coming up with good ways to solve those particular problems.

Then she remembered something else about Trudy. A few days after dividing the jellybeans, Louise had overheard Trudy and her friends feverishly discussing Trudy's upcoming birthday party. It seems Trudy's mother had given her one hundred dollars to use on the party and told her it was up to her to decide how to spend the money. The girls were trying to decide on a plan for spending the money. They had agreed that the party required cupcakes, bubble tea, materials to decorate T-shirts, and, they hoped, tickets to use the local skating rink. But did they have enough money to do what they wanted? And which cupcakes (and how many) would they be able to buy? One friend, Zelda, said, "If we invite everyone on the list, we can't get enough good stuff for the T-shirts." She had clearly done some mental calculations.

The other girl, Alice, said, "We don't even know how much the T-shirt stuff is gonna cost." More good thinking.

Trudy was getting exasperated. "Let's just buy what we need and see how it comes out."

Louise now realized that she should have spent a little more time trying to understand the way Trudy thought and that the clues were there in Trudy's more casual activities and conversation. Louise's friend, Fred, who taught sixth-grade math, said that whenever he sat down with a kid who was stumped, he suggested the child start by saying whatever it was he noticed about the numbers or problems in front of him. He wanted his input to begin with what the child knew and thought, not with what he wanted the child to know and think eventually. He'd say to a child, "Tell me just one thing you notice about these two numbers." His student might notice the thing he hoped he would (for instance, "This number can be divided by that number"). But often the student would notice something else altogether. That was fine by Fred. Getting students to make their own observations was always the best first step. And it gave him a window onto their thinking.

Trudy could envision spending the money; she had the mental skills to play that scenario out in her head. She could also envision the underlying problem that the money might not buy everything they needed. But she couldn't see that it would be possible, by calculating various scenarios, and using division and multiplication, to work out which scenario made the most sense. She could only imagine that if she took the money and began to go from shop to shop, she'd get what she wanted, until she ran out. She was hampered by her difficulty with imagining different components and how they might fit together. She had a perfectly reasonable plan, and if she had been, say, five, it would have made a lot of sense. But by fourth grade, we hope children are using their ability to think a scenario through and mentally manipulate the various elements of that scenario. Though the early stages of talking, planning, and envisioning come naturally to children everywhere, those mental skills expand and become refined to do things like higher mathematics only under certain circumstances.

Giles, another colleague of Louise's, told the following story. "I had a child in my class called Zahra. She had a total block on division. The class was talking about planning school trips and how many buses they would need to get all the children on. I set out the problem for them like this: If there are 268 children and the buses each hold 17 seats, how many buses do you think we'll need to take? The children were supposed to work out that you couldn't leave any children behind. Even if you had 15 full buses, you'd still need 1 for the extra 13 kids that didn't fit on the others. Zahra could do the first part of the division but was totally flummoxed by the problem of the remaining children. I'd ask what she would do with the remainder and she'd look at me and go, 'Add it? Divide it again?' She had no understanding of the physical need for an extra bus for extra children.

"We worked through about six of these questions and she still wasn't getting it. So we used cubes as children and arranged them into fifteen-seater bus formations in cardboard boxes, and when it got to the three remaining children, I asked Zahra what we should do with them. She thought about it for a minute and then she said, 'Let's put them on the half-empty bus.' That totally confused me. I was sure she was gonna say, 'Let's get another box.' So I said, 'What half-empty bus?' She pointed back to her book and said, 'Well in the last question we did, there were only four children on the last bus, so let's put these three on that bus.' Somehow she thought the two word problems could be fused the way two teachers might combine forces and share all of the buses. She could work with the numbers, and she could work with the boxes, but somehow the underlying ideas continued to elude her."

Workbooks Versus Thinking

When we think of what children learn in school, we tend to think of things like getting better at solving algebra problems, analyzing literary passages, and identifying important events in history. But actually, those very specific skills rest on more fundamental thought processes. For example, algebra rests on understanding the relationships between the whole and its parts, literary analysis depends on imagining a world conjured only through words, and history depends on the ability to imagine changing around various components of a sequence so that the outcome of an event might be radically different. Those more fundamental, powerful thought processes do not begin when children get to school and encounter problems in workbooks and quizzes. They begin earlier, in much messier and more complex everyday experiences.

What Real Thinking Looks Like

Consider a nonmath example, the all-important ability to think counterfactually. We draw on this skill every time we think about hypotheticals (What would have happened if Hitler had won World War II? What will happen if we add H_2O to this mixture of liquids and solids and leave it overnight? What might happen if we use single payer insurance? What would have happened if Martin Luther King, Jr. had not been assassinated? and so on). The ability to think about how things might have turned out given alternative events, or how things might turn out in the future under various scenarios, is one of the capacities that sets us apart from all other species. Children of two cannot engage in such thinking. Their thoughts are still too rooted in the here and now. And yet, they begin working on this foundational skill when they engage in pretend play. Imagine, for a moment, the child who asks her mommy to play Wonder Woman with her. She says, "This time, you try to knock me down and I'll leap over you and get away." Once they've acted that out, she says, "OK. Let's do it again. But this time, I'll grab your arms and tie you up. Then I won't get away; you'll be my prisoner." By replaying the scenario over and over

The ability to think about how things might have turned out given alternative events, or how things might turn out in the future under various scenarios, is one of the capacities that sets us apart from all other species.

again, revising various pieces each time, she is practicing counterfactual thinking. Once in school, this capacity, brought to bear on other material, and done mentally rather than in play, becomes a cornerstone of what it means to be a thinker. It allows us to think not only about the way the world is but also about how it might be under various circumstances. We need that kind of thinking in medicine, in science, in politics, in engineering, and in any situation where we are called upon to figure out a solution to a problem for which straightforward tinkering won't work and we can't simply follow someone else's procedures or instructions.

There are other fundamental thinking skills that begin early in life and can, under the right circumstances, expand and strengthen at school. Take, for example, the ability to think like a scientist. Most children love the natural world. They don't need a classroom for that. They need opportunities to explore the plants and animals around them. They also tend to be interested in any number of scientific principles on display in everyday life. Why do some things melt and other things harden when heated? Why can some babies walk right away (horses and cows) and others cannot? And within the first year, they are already practicing the fine art of hypothesis testing. And yet, babies are not the same as well-educated scientists. They need some help to get there.

An Example of How Teachers Can Build on Children's Intuition

No matter how much freedom children are given to explore the world around them and use their own innate ability to test hypotheses, there are certain kinds of thinking they don't come to on their own. For example, few children will figure out one of the pillars of all good scientific work: holding variables constant. For instance, imagine a group of children is trying to make a car out of wood and spools and other everyday items. They want to figure out how to make it roll down a ramp quickly. They keep tinkering with the parts that can be changed: the material of the wheels, the size of the wheels, and the length of the car's body. Sometimes the car goes down quickly and other times it doesn't. They note this, but they still don't know which feature is critical to making the car go faster or slower. Another child comes up to them and says, "I'm gonna make one too. What makes it go fast?" The children shrug. They have no idea, because they keep changing more than one thing at a time. To understand science (whether in order to do an experiment yourself or to comprehend the results of other people's experiments), you need to be so familiar with this principle that every time it's violated, you balk. Learning it doesn't come naturally to most children. It takes time, practice, and the guidance of more experienced scientists to learn it.

Though researchers don't agree about how explicit a teacher should be in pointing out this critical aspect of good experiments, they *do* agree that children can learn it and must. And yet it is rarely the central focus of elementary school science curricula. Many well-regarded science textbooks for fourth grade contain a lot of interesting topics for kids to learn about: how plants react to light, what chlorophyll and photosynthesis are, and how to decide if a plant needs more water. The books also take students step-by-step through a variety of small, fun experiments. But in doing that, they miss explaining exactly the thing children need most: how to pose a question so that it can be answered with data, how to collect data that will answer that question with some precision, and how to interpret messy, complicated data—in other words, how to do what scientists do. Children have been engaging in the building blocks of that intellectual work from infancy. They are born with the impulse to find out, but they need guidance to hone that into the powerful set of intellectual tools we call science. However, even at school, children cannot learn to think like scientists simply by following instructions or learning facts. They have to actually engage in scientific experimentation and thinking, with guidance from more experienced scientists. They also need feedback highlighting the underlying principles they are practicing. Many teachers do these same things as they help children become writers.

The Singular Power of Writing

Another important kind of thinking that begins early in life is the ability to construct a coherent argument. This fundamental skill is valuable in two ways: First, it allows you to convince others of your point of view and communicate not only with those who know and trust you but also those who don't know you and have little reason to trust you. Secondly, it helps you organize and make sense of your ideas and experiences.

Psychologist Michael Halliday (1973) argued that children use language for two essential functions: to think and to communicate. Spoken language is the foundation on which more mature thinking skills are built. The most powerful way to help young children prepare to be good writers and good thinkers is to encourage a lot of conversation. But once in school, that's not enough. A child might be a powerful communicator with his friends, able to convince them to play what he wants, to like one friend and not another, and to listen while he tells stories of what happened to him over the weekend. Good raconteurs are born every day, and all kinds of family settings nurture such oratorical skills. But by the time children are in elementary school, those skills can carry them only so far; they need to be good writers to go farther. And it turns out that writing is not simply a matter of putting what you say out loud down on the page. Writing requires some new and different intellectual moves. For one thing, writing doesn't afford repetition and redundancy in the way talking does. Writers cannot use facial expressions, tone of voice, or movements to underscore their words. Instead, to write well, one must convey enough information so that the reader gets it without all those support systems. If you are unclear when you talk, you may see confusion on your listener's face, and you can go back and repair. Not so with writing. Lots and lots of conversation is key to the development of literacy, but there's more to it than that.

Psychologist Catherine Snow (2010) argues that when children learn to write, they acquire certain intellectual strengths they cannot get any other way. They develop the ability to back their point up with information, to lay their idea out in a clear, logical sequence, and to include information that the reader must have in order to comprehend what they are saying. But her research goes further than this. She has shown that simply teaching children the mechanics of a proper essay doesn't do the trick. In one study, she asked sixth graders to choose a topic to debate about from a list of personally meaningful topics (whether lunch period should be lengthened, for instance). She gave the students a week to prepare their written arguments before the debate. The students' vocabularies, clarity, organization, and use of information were much stronger than those of students who had been given the same information and asked to write essays. So it turns out that writing helps people think *and* communicate, but learning to write requires *wanting* to think and communicate, which includes caring about the topic and the audience for whom you are writing.

Everyone writes with greater force and clarity when they care about what they are writing and when they care about their audience.

Consider, for instance, assigning children to write an essay on Komodo dragons or the Civil Rights Movement, giving them a clear rubric about how you will grade their papers and some helpful rules about how to structure their papers. Even if you give them a chance to make a drawing or a diorama to liven up the assignment, they will be writing their essay to show you what they know about lizards or civil rights. Contrast this with, say, asking your students to write a letter to their local paper convincing the town to throw a party at the end of the school year, or a mystery novel for other children to read. In one case, at least some of the children will try to follow the rules and include the necessary information. They want to please the teacher or get a good grade. But in the second assignment, the words may well gush out of them, the order and sentences taking shape as they think about what they want their readers to know or feel.

Teachers are often encouraged to teach children the mechanics of writing as a set of disembodied rules. They understandably assume that if children master those rules, they will someday be able and want to write interesting, coherent descriptions and arguments. But the process unfolds in the opposite direction. Children naturally like to think and talk, and as they get older this urge can provide them with a very efficient platform for writing. When children feel some urgency about their topic, their message, or their audience, they can more easily make the leap from talking to writing. That, in turn, can help them become better thinkers.

Ben, a first-grade teacher, says about his class, "My goal for first grade is to help them learn how to be with one another, how to really listen, and to become readers and writers. To do those things well pretty much takes up the whole year. In the long run, it's worth it. Because if they are readers and writers, they will become thinkers." He tells the following story, to illustrate how he works.

> *Children naturally like to think and talk, and as they get older this urge can provide them with a very efficient platform for writing. When children feel some urgency about their topic, their message or their audience, they can more easily make the leap from talking to writing. That, in turn, can help them become better thinkers.*

"Lilly was articulate, social, athletic, and very funny. She was an awesome reader, loved books, and had a great conceptual understanding of all things math, especially for how numbers work. For some reason, though, her writing was not at the same level as everything else. She mastered the mechanics of it right away and had no trouble thinking of what to write about, but her stories were mostly sparse and disorganized. She put plenty of creativity and detail in her drawings, but struggled to create a picture with her words for the reader to see and follow.

"I give lots of opportunities for students to tell their stories out loud before, during, and after writing them. Lilly often told rich, extended stories orally, so my first strategy was to work with her to create a bridge from the spoken to the written. Lilly's parents are from Central America and Spanish was her first language, so I wondered if there was a language element at play that I didn't understand. I also consulted with our speech/language teacher to explore ideas around expressive language. I tried some outlining, sequencing, and vocabulary strategies. They helped Lilly add detail and transitions, but nothing really resonated and her stories still didn't come to life.

"Meanwhile, I was really happy to see Lilly had become best friends with Maude, another girl in the class. There is a whole other story about Maude. She is very shy and quiet and I worked all year to find ways to help her gain confidence. She would go entire days without speaking even if I asked her a direct question. We shared a notebook back and forth. It was like a diary where she wrote about things she did and thought about, so I was getting to know her a little. I was thrilled to see Lilly and Maude interacting. Because Maude is so soft-spoken, I could never hear what they were saying, but I was hopeful that their conversations, like the notebook, would help Maude build momentum for talking in other situations too.

"Then finally one day I overheard Lilly telling Maude about the monkey bars. She was explaining step-by-step how to climb up, hold on, swing your feet, and grab on to the next bar. It was the perfect tutorial. You know, a teacher is always looking for clues. That's when I got the idea for her to write how-to books. I asked her to write down what she was telling Maude so everyone could learn it. From there, she did the tooth brushing one [see Figure 2–1], how to ride a bike, how to tie your shoes, how to make tacos, even how to write a how-to book!"

FIGURE 2-1 *Lilly's How-to Book*

How to bruse your teeh.
Step one. get your tush brus.
Step tow. pote tushpaste
on the tush bruse.

Teny pote the tuse bruse
your mohe. Step four. Bruse it
allaronde. Tany gaved a
cup.

Pote woter in the cup.
Spite the woter in the
seink. Tany flose.

Teny twrow the fose away.

Two things about this story stand out. First is Ben's casual yet profound comment that a teacher is always looking for clues. Ben knew that if Lilly were to become a better writer and thinker, he would need to pay close attention to her likes, her dislikes, her skills, her interests, and the way her mind worked. The second remarkable thing about it is the way in which that one small essay transformed her from a chaotic thinker into a clear thinker. She could not have done that without writing about something she knew well and liked a lot. It also made a huge difference that she was writing *for* someone she knew well and liked a lot. The key to the success of that assignment was Ben's ability to think about Lilly and connect that to his real educational goal—to help Lilly become a reader and a writer, so that she could become a thinker. He had realized that Lilly's path to thinking would take her through a stretch of how-to books. This had little to do with a curriculum guide, or a lesson plan, and everything to do with understanding what the development of thinking involves.

The human capacity for thought is breathtaking. Some might argue it's the most important capacity we have. To become good at all kinds of thinking (not just planning your dinner or figuring out how to get from one town to another), children need opportunities to actually think. Thinking is not the same thing as practicing the isolated skills that might, in some cases, be helpful for specific academic tasks.

A Shift from Skills to Problem-Solving

A year had passed. Soon Louise would be seeing Cora at Thanksgiving. She finally had at least part of the answer to Cora's question. And she had begun to reconsider her colorful and well-organized classroom. Perhaps she had given too much attention to teaching children specific academic skills and not quite enough attention to giving them opportunities to think. Like teachers everywhere, she had, without realizing it, accepted the conventional wisdom that by learning how to add and subtract, answer problems concerning place value, punctuate properly, memorize vocabulary, and identify the parts of the cell, children would be armed with the tools for good thinking. And though tools like those are useful to thinkers, practicing them doesn't *lead* to good thinking. The first steps of good thinking are formed before children even get to school, when they are playing, helping out, and talking with others. Talking to dad while riding to school, helping a brother set the table, and playing Wonder Woman or building blocks with a sister all share two common factors. The first is that such activities are intrinsically interesting. No one has to convince a child to speculate about why some animals keep moving after they've been killed or the circumstances under which bigger blocks can be balanced on top of smaller blocks. No one needs to explain to a child that setting the table is a way to learn about one-to-one correspondences, and certainly no one needs to convince a child to make up stories, build buildings, sort toys, or analyze riveting origin myths (like Spider-Man's). The second factor all these activities share is that the intellectual skills they require and enhance are deeply embedded, invisibly so, in everyday engaging and meaningful activities.

One of the biggest shifts classrooms require of children is the shift from the kinds of informal learning-in-context that happens at home and in the neighborhood to the more formal, decontextualized kinds of learning required at school. And though individual skills that aid thinking can and sometimes should be learned outside of a particular context, good thinking almost always occurs within a meaningful context. Someone has to want to solve a problem, come up with an idea, or consider someone else's idea, or has to be interested in the specific topic, to think well and to get better at thinking.

Children won't ever all think the same way. Thank goodness. Some will be more inventive than others, some smarter than others. Some seem to talk through problems, and others tend to visualize their ideas (which has nothing to do with the idea of different intelligences, just the variety of ways children and adults approach the world intellectually). Some do their best thinking in the company of others, and some think best when alone. Some think by writing how-to books!

Children won't ever all think the same way. Thank goodness.

It takes time and experience to become a good thinker. Most of the important components of good thinking are not the ones learned in textbooks, but the ones learned from engaging in real thinking, in the company of good thinkers. What kinds of experiences demand real thinking from children? Activities that they care about—ones that are sufficiently complex and have a goal that matters to them. The best thinking comes when a child is trying to solve a problem. The problem might be concrete and useful: how to build a space ship with blocks, how to get ants to change their route in a maze or how to build a transistor radio. The problem might be how to explain phenomena or convince someone else of one's argument: how to convince others that there is no climate change, how to save water, whether everyone should be subjected to the same rules, and how to explain differences between species, to give just a few examples. But remember, when children are little their thinking advances in remarkable ways not because they feel they must improve their cognitive skills, but because they see the world in ever more complex ways, and as they see new, more challenging intellectual problems in the world around them, they feel the urge to come up with equally sophisticated solutions. In other words, given a rich physical and intellectual environment, children notice the things that fit their way of thinking. Based on what they notice, they construct or choose problems that fit their intellectual capacities. However, no child experiences the world of problems and solutions on her own. From day one, children think in the company of others. It may be blocks, fish tanks, pizza slices, and weather changes that draw children in, but we know from research that what a child notices, or even sees as an interesting problem, is shaped in part by the adults around her.

The kinds of intellectual strategies children use are deeply influenced by the things adults ask, point out, and suggest. This informal kind of input often has a deeper impact on children's underlying thinking skills than the more superficial knowledge imparted through direct instruction. This point is important and controversial. An extended example might help.

Imagine a classroom in which the teacher wants children to learn several academic skills appropriate to the fourth grade: place value, long division, the basics of measuring mass and volume, the elements of a clear sentence, and the components of narrative structure. Perhaps she has a set of worksheets and related activities for each of those skills. She introduces one of the activities like this: "Today we're going to learn about long division with three-digit numbers. You'll need this a lot as you get older. Someone might ask you to hike the Appalachian Trail with them and say she wants to travel 637 miles in three weeks. You might want to figure out how many miles you'll have to walk each day. So you'll have to do some long division!" Then she puts the problem on the board and asks the children how they would go about solving it. She invites their ideas, refraining from praise or criticism and instead simply encouraging them to think out loud. After a few minutes, she asks if anyone knows the proper steps to solving a long division problem. One child gets up and shows how it's done. The teacher congratulates her student and then indicates which parts of the student's work are correct and which are not. She then goes over the logic of the procedure. She hands out a worksheet with five similar problems, telling the children they have the next thirty minutes to complete the sheet. Imagine now she structures something similar for all the skills she wants her students to master.

These are reasonable lessons. She starts with what seems like an appealing example and gives kids a chance to take a stab at it, but she doesn't let them spend too much time doing things the wrong way. She doesn't want them to get entrenched in faulty thinking. Instead she quickly shows them the correct way to proceed. Finally she gives them a chance to practice their new skills. With this approach, some of the kids will in fact become adept at long division. But there is little evidence that in doing so, they will actually become better thinkers. What would work better? An understanding of how thinking changes between the ages of four and twelve provides a road map for how one might go about coming up with activities that have a more transformative impact.

Imagine a second classroom scenario. A teacher invites a small group of children to sit at table on which lies a small and somewhat messy heap of materials. The heap contains some screws, bolts, tape, wire, empty wooden spools, and a variety of mysterious small objects, all gathered from the children's kitchen drawers, the ones that nearly every family has into which they toss all manner of items, useful and otherwise. The teacher says, "Can you all make something useful with this? You have an hour a day, for the next week or two. Let me know when you feel you're done." She spends the next two weeks taking a seat at each table, offering suggestions, noticing interesting features of their processes and what they are building, listening to them talk to one another, pointing out weaknesses, and asking questions about what they've made, what they want to make, and what obstacles they are facing. In short, she is the master problem solver, letting the apprentices do their work, offering periodic help, and sometimes challenging them to think in just slightly more complex ways than they are on their own. In the first example, the child is learning procedures. In the second example, instead of learning a long division procedure, the student would learn how to think something through, from beginning to end. A child who really knows how to think something through can, at some point, learn the set of rules that make long division efficient and accurate and apply those rules when needed. The procedure becomes a tool in the service of real problem solving.

That is just one example. There are examples like that for mathematics, science, and history. The point is that Louise realized that to help her kids become good thinkers, she needed to make fewer posters, activity centers, and cool worksheets, no matter how attractive. Instead she decided to create more opportunities for her students to embark on tasks that invited them to think. She needed to try to spend more time as the master thinker—hinting, suggesting, asking, and modeling. To do that, she needed to make sure was a good thinker herself. Here too, the research on early development paved the way for her. Children who are around those who interpret, ask questions, draw connections, think backward, and question data are more likely to do so themselves. No worksheets, no matter how lively or pretty, can replace the input of thoughtful, smart adults. Interesting problems, time to solve them, informal guidance and challenge from thoughtful adults who notice the thought processes of their students—these are the ingredients that build on a child's inherent drive to think in ever more powerful ways.

Louise decided she would figure out how to model the rest of her curriculum on the robotics program she had developed. Kids would be trying to solve complicated problems that interested and delighted them. They'd work with others. They'd take time, and mistakes and missteps would be valuable parts of the process. They'd have to use a mixture of hands-on, active thinking-in-context and more reflective, abstract, bookish kinds of thinking. The children would know when their efforts were successful, not because of the number of right answers, but because they had come up with a solution to whatever problem they had set out to solve. The room might not look as neat and pretty. But it would be a beehive of intellectual activity.

CHAPTER THREE

Was Grace Lonely?

———— ◆ ————

Friendships ⋆ Peer Rejection and Neglect ⋆
Social Development

NINA WASN'T VERY worried. Just a little. Each morning, she and her eight-year-old daughter Grace walked to school together, four blocks from their apartment. Grace would chatter away the whole time. She'd recount her dreams, comment on other children's footwear, and theorize about the television show they had watched together the night before. Grace had lots to say about everything. In fact, sometimes it seemed like she would never run out of words. As they walked through the school gate, Grace always seemed to know the parent greeter for that day and would wave in a friendly, easy way. Grace would give her mother a goodbye hug in the playground and head to her third-grade classroom, loping on her long skinny legs and large feet. But as Nina watched her daughter disappear from the bright West Coast sunshine into the shady classroom, she noticed that Grace was the only little girl who walked into the building alone. All the other girls seemed to meet up with one or two other children in the playground and make their entrance to the school day together, often arm in arm. Nina thought to herself, "That's OK; Grace has friends. It's not like she drags her feet about coming to school. She's fine."

When Nina came home from work at the end of the day, Grace would be curved into the pillows of their small couch, lost in a book. She'd look over her shoulder, smile breezily at Nina, and then turn back to her book. When Nina would ask if

Grace had any homework, Grace would call out, "Finished it! Easy-cheesy," and return to her reading. At dinnertime when Nina would ask Grace about her school day, Grace would launch into a detailed discussion of her project on the Mission Rafael—what the girls there wore, how they cooked, and the beautiful poster she was making of their village. Nina would ask, "Anything else?"

Grace would dive in again, this time offering a long recitative of another little girl who never seemed to listen when their teacher, Ms. Guthrie, was talking. "I mean, it's not like she's rude or anything. But I don't think she's a very good student. I don't know why Ms. Guthrie doesn't get mad at her. I feel like I wanna tell her she should just *pay attention*."

Nina would try to ignore Grace's impulse to be a know-it-all. Instead, she'd prod a bit further: "And how was lunchtime?"

"Yech," Grace would answer. "The sandwich was mushy. I don't like it when you put tomato in it. It gets yucky. But I ate the carrots."

Nina would persist. "Who'd you eat with?"

Grace would say, nonchalantly, "Oh, Ms. Rivera, in the library. We always eat together." A faint cloud would form in Nina's mind. Why did Grace hang out with the librarian instead of the other kids?

Periodically, when the cloud hung too heavy in Nina's brain, she'd say to Grace, "Would you like to invite a few of your friends over on Friday? We could have an ice cream party."

But Grace would shrug and say, "Nah. Mrs. Jenkins said I could come next door and we would make cupcakes together. I'm gonna do that." It seemed to Nina as if Grace didn't really have a group of friends to invite over. When Nina thought about it, she realized that the only kids Grace played with on the weekends were the children who lived on her street, the kids she had known all her life, from family picnics. Why wasn't she making new friends in school?

Finally, in October, when it was time for her parent-teacher conference, Nina couldn't push the cloud away anymore. She sat down at the low table across from Ms. Guthrie, smiled uncertainly, and then blurted out, "Does Grace have any friends at school?"

Ms. Guthrie, a seasoned teacher, paused for a minute and then said gently, "Why do you ask?"

Nina answered, the corners of her mouth tightening with tension, "Grace keeps saying she eats lunch in the library. And at recess, same thing. It sounds like she would always rather be in the classroom with you, or with the librarian, than with friends. I mean, I know she gets along with other kids. She's always had friends at home. But maybe, I don't know, are kids here mean to her?"

Ms. Guthrie had heard some version of this question countless times over the years. But that worry hadn't always been so common. During her own childhood in Oregon, grown-ups seemed fairly oblivious to the social dynamics of seven- and eight-year-olds. In those days, and during her time in graduate school, teachers worried about whether their students were learning their math facts, how to read, and how to write in cursive, and about how to maintain order in the classroom. Then, in the eighties, the big talk had turned to children's self-esteem. Everyone was worried that too many children felt bad about themselves, that they needed help building their confidence (Galen and Underwood 1997). Teachers were encouraged to find techniques to boost children's confidence, making sure that each child felt good about him- or herself. The assumption was that if kids felt assured and happy with themselves, they would get along better with others and do better academically. But as the research unfolded, it turned out that pumping up children's sense of self-worth by telling them how terrific they were not only didn't really help them win friends or improve academically but could make them more aggressive and difficult to be around. Inflated pride was not helping, but perhaps there were ways to ensure that more children actually *were* successful, more of the time (Underwood, Galen, and Paquette 2001).

Teachers were now advised to structure lessons so that every child could actually *be* successful, rather than just *feel* successful. The idea was to give each student work that was just a little bit beyond his or her capacity—enough so that children would have to stretch academically, but not fail. Across the country, teachers became more adept at tailoring lessons to provide just the right amount of challenge for each of their students. Research based on Lev Vygotsky's theory of the zone of proximal development (Vygotsky 1980), combined with research such as Patricia Greenfield's on the ways in which adults intuitively challenge children, showed that fine-tuning of this sort does help children learn more (Greenfield 1984). It's one of several excellent ways to make sure children are getting what we want them to from a lesson. But such scaffolding didn't turn out to have much broader impact on children. The enthusiasm for pumping up children's self-esteem gradually waned.

Then in the mid-nineties, psychologists and educators began to worry about a new concern. It seemed that problems *between* children had become the educational mystery of the day. This concern was fueled in part by reports of cruel bullying on the playground (Blatchford, Pellegrini, and Baines 2015). As the Internet wormed its way into the social lives of children, two things changed. Children could chat with one another far after the school day had ended. Even in suburbs, where children might not gather on the stoop or playground, it seemed they were talking to one another, sharing images, and playing online games together, late into the

Once social platforms for children entered the scene, children's exchanges with one another usually entailed an audience—peers could spectate one another's activity, commenting and injecting their views. Sometimes the comments became as important a form of social interaction as the original exchange between a few children. In this way, online socializing radically altered the dynamic of childhood friendships. What had been fairly private now became widely public.

evening. The Internet didn't merely allow children to spend more time with friends. Its effect was more insidious than that. Once social platforms for children entered the scene, children's exchanges with one another usually entailed an audience—peers could spectate one another's activity, commenting and injecting their views. Sometimes the comments became as important a form of social interaction as the original exchange between a few children. In this way, online socializing radically altered the dynamic of childhood friendships. What had been fairly private now became widely public. Whether the Internet increased the intensity or frequency of bullying, or just made it more apparent to adults, it underlined the social problems that children grapple with. As the new century unfolded, friendships and the perils of social life, even in elementary school, became the predominant worry of parents and teachers alike. Researchers such as Marion Underwood, John Coie, Nicki Crick, Debra Pepler, and Dan Olweus have shown that the ways in which children make friends, as well as the ways in which they hurt one another's feelings, follow predictable patterns.

As Nina sat across from Ms. Guthrie, all she could conjure up was the image of her little Gracey, sitting alone in the library, looking out the window at all the other children gathered in small groups to chat or play kickball and hula-hoop. She knew her child seemed separate from the others during the school day. It was so painful to think about, and even more painful to imagine how Grace must feel—isolated and solitary, on her own in the playground, at lunch, and during gym. Nina couldn't get beyond that sad image.

Ms. Guthrie, on the other hand, had seen enough children over the years to know that there was more than one way of being isolated, and when it comes to trying to help such a child, the differences matter. Ms. Guthrie said to Nina, "Let me pay more attention for a few days, and then I'll get back to you."

Nina thought to herself, "Pay attention? What have you been doing all these weeks? Didn't you realize my child was being persecuted?" But that's not what she said. She said, "OK. *When* will you get back to me?"

If you ask most teachers to tell you about the social dynamics in their classroom, they can give you a pretty detailed and accurate rundown of which kids are in charge, who is left out, and who hangs out together. But adults only get one version of the social dramas unfolding in their midst. Lots goes on that they don't know about. For instance, by middle childhood, some children (more typically the boys) still tend to taunt and challenge one another in vivid and often physical ways. But other children (usually girls) tend to find more circuitous and hidden means for social combat. They try to win favor, exclude someone, and gain dominance via others in the group. Psychologists label these indirect strategies *relational aggression*. For instance, one girl might tell another girl that their mutual friend said mean things about her. By passing on hurtful information she sows seeds of dislike and hurt, and when it works, it leaves her in a stronger position with each of the other two. But because this all happens via quiet comments and private conversations, teachers can easily miss what's going on.

Sometimes teachers don't see even the more obvious signs of conflict between kids, for the simple reason that children are tougher on one another when grown-ups aren't watching. When Canadian researchers Wendy Craig and Debra Pepler (1998) installed a video camera on the playground in elementary schools and filmed recess, they found that there were, on average, over 4.5 episodes of aggression per hour. Kids were saying and doing things to one another that they would never do during the other parts of the school day when the teacher was nearby. It's hard to know about behaviors that you can't, for one reason or another, see. Plus, not all of those behaviors are a real problem.

Hitting, taunting, and gossiping among kids are not, in and of themselves, serious warning signs of bigger trouble. After all, a certain degree of aggression between children is completely normal. Forming alliances, resolving conflicts, and working out subtle social hierarchies is an important part of the work of childhood. In fact, conflicts are not only normal but healthy. By and large children are resilient to squabbles or ruptures, even slightly upsetting or painful ones. A kid who has a friend or group of friends is likely to argue with her buddies and also periodically cross others she isn't all that close to. Thus, simply tracking the frequency of aggression a child or group of children engages in doesn't really help a teacher figure out who is in the thick of it socially, who is at the far margins of the group, and how kids feel about one another. However, in recent years, researchers have devised an ingenious method for peering into the inner social dynamics of children.

Sociometrics is a relatively recent method for learning how children feel about one another (Eisenberg et al. 1993). This method provides a numerical map of the social dynamics within a given classroom. To gather such information, researchers invite children within a classroom to identify whom they most like or want to play with (these questions obviously elicit related but different kinds of information) and whom they least like or want to play with. Sometimes researchers also ask the children to rate how each of their peers is viewed by the group; thus they learn who is liked and who isn't, but they can also gauge the social reputation of each child. Even very young children, it turns out, know the difference between whom they actually want to spend time with and who seems to be popular or powerful within the larger group.

Some children get high ratings from all of their classmates—they are liked and admired by many. Even kids who aren't good friends with such a child recognize his or her social capital. Then there are the kids who are disliked or feared by nearly everyone. Often such kids are aggressive, difficult to get along with, and sometimes unappealing in other ways. But the social world of children is more complex even than that. A teacher can usually tell who is the queen bee and who is wearing a perpetual "Kick Me" sign. But there is a vast middle ground that is less obvious. In every classroom there are likely to be at least a few kids who don't get particularly high or low scores on sociometric scales. Such a child is never mentioned when the kids are asked, "Whom would you most like to play with?" or "Whom do the other kids really like?" and they may not consistently be at the bottom of everyone's list either. No one thinks of them as kids to fear or tease. They aren't loved and they aren't hated. They're just ignored. And that can be quite painful and bode poorly for a child's future. Was Grace one of those kids?

Grace was a good student and so likeable—to teachers, that is. But what did other children think about her? When Ms. Guthrie thought it over, she realized she hadn't really paid much attention to Grace's social interactions, so she didn't really know whether Nina was onto something or just getting herself in a lather because Grace liked the library. She'd need to observe Grace in a more systematic way. But what should she pay attention to? She decided she'd start by identifying Grace's friends. Maybe Ms. Guthrie should take it as a clue that she didn't know them off the top of her head, because with most kids she could instantly tell you who their best buddies were.

When she assigned kids to work in pairs, it was always easy to choose a partner for Grace. She never worried that there would be fighting. The other kids never objected to Grace as a work buddy. When she thought about seating arrangements, she couldn't quite remember whom Grace typically chose to sit next to.

Suddenly, Ms. Guthrie wasn't so sure she knew whether Grace had friends or not. What would she look for as a sign that someone was really Grace's good pal? She needed to think a bit about what it means to have a friend when you are eight.

The ABCs of Friendship

No one thinks of babies as having friends. Put two one-year-olds side by side in a sandbox, and they might ignore one another or they might watch one another with interest for a while. But they are unlikely to coordinate their play or engage in much deliberate collaboration. But that quickly changes. By two or three children seek others out, coordinate their play with others, and interact in all kinds of ways— work near one another, announce plans for building, digging, and imagining to one another, argue, laugh, transgress, offer sympathy, and copy each other. But those first friendships are often fleeting.

At first, kids tend to love the ones they're with. Most make friends quickly and easily, jumping into every manner of play—establishing pretend scenarios involving superheroes, hospitals, restaurants, and bad guys, building with blocks or sticks and leaves, digging in the sand or dirt, organizing games like soccer and hopscotch, and inventing endless varieties of competition. Watch the edge of any Little League field anywhere in the country, and you will see the younger siblings find their way toward one another, as if drawn by magnets, as they establish endless forms of fleeting connection. But they also soon begin to show preferences for particular children.

Just think of the neighborhood park. Toddlers leap out of their strollers and rush over to the slide, swing set, or sandbox and march right over to the same child, day after day. Researchers have shown that by eighteen months, placed in a room of same-age children (say, at day care), a child will touch the child she seeks for a friend more than she touches the other children, will talk more to her, smile more, and make more friendly gestures. Most children are drawn

Most children are drawn to others their own age, seeking, as we do for the rest of our lives, the stimulation, comfort, and affirmation of similar people. Time with friends offers some surprising long-term benefits to young children.

to others their own age, seeking, as we do for the rest of our lives, the stimulation, comfort, and affirmation of similar people. Time with friends offers some surprising long-term benefits to young children (Dunn 2004).

When preschoolers are playing with a real friend, as opposed to someone they happen to be paired with on the playground, they are more likely to pretend together. When you think about it, making things up together requires a great deal of coordination. In order for two or more children to pretend, they have to interpret one another's redesignation of objects (the hairbrush becomes a telephone; the stick becomes a magic wand), as well as the meaning of various symbolic gestures (when the other child flaps her arms, she's flying, and when she makes staccato noises with her mouth, she's shooting). To play together they have to construct a shared imaginary world, and that's no small feat, requiring all kinds of tacit agreements, perspective taking, and fine-tuning. It's much harder to do if you don't feel close to the other person.

But it's not just that friends collaborate better with one another than they do with peers who are not friends. They also disagree more frequently with genuine friends, and those disagreements are every bit as valuable as the more cooperative aspects of their play. Just like adults, young children are more likely to argue with a friend than a nonfriend. But they're also more likely to work it out—to talk, to figure out a compromise, to share, and to resolve things before moving on. In other words, giving children a chance, in school, to make friends and then spend time with those friends provides them with unique and essential opportunities to learn how to collaborate, negotiate conflict, and resolve disputes.

How do children so young choose their friendships? The same way we do: they prefer someone similar. They gravitate toward children who are as intellectually mature as they and have about the same level of cooperation skills. Young children who grab things from other children, have trouble sharing, or are aggressive in the playground tend to match up with other kids with antisocial behavior. Kids magically seem to choose friends who are about as well liked as they are and as gregarious or reticent as they. In other words, from early on, we try to find friends who match us on key dimensions of personality and maturity.

As they begin to choose particular friends, they also acquire a sense of what it means to have a friend. By four most can identify their "best friend" and will describe that person in more positive terms than other children, even the ones with whom they are friends. At this point they know the difference between buddy and good friend, even if Tuesday's buddy is Thursday's best friend and vice versa. Their social categories are forming.

Three- and four-year-olds base their friendships on what both children like to do together (build with blocks, play soccer, or make up pretend scenarios). By third grade though, kids' friendships are thicker and more multifaceted. A fairly simple pleasure in the same activities has been replaced by a mutual need for intimacy—a friend is someone you feel you really know and who knows you. By nine years old or so, friends know enough about one another to actually have some sense of shared history. They reminisce together and argue about the past. They also begin to know about one another's lives. Revealing inner feelings, telling stories about what has happened at home, and disclosing secrets becomes central to the friendship. But age isn't the only source of variation in friendships.

Boys and Girls

Somewhere during this transition, gender begins to matter (Underwood 2007). Boys and girls, on the whole, follow different paths when it comes to close friends; boys are more likely to continue establishing closeness through shared activity, while girls make more of a shift from activity to talk. Girls disclose more to one another than boys do. And, as described earlier, they handle aggression differently. Boys boast, challenge one another, and easily fall into various forms of straightforward battling. Girls are more likely to battle one another indirectly, telling stories behind one another's backs, cultivating a friendship as a means of hurting another girl, and reporting mean comments from one to another. But there is plenty of overlap as well. Both boys and girls know much more about their close friends than they do about other children—not just what they like to do and eat, but what they are good at, what has happened to them in the past, and what their family lives are like. Friendships are good for children, but they also feel good. Children crave friends, and a happy lunch or recess with buddies is worth far more than an A on a spelling test. By the same token, a rupture in a friendship or expulsion from the group can cause much greater pain than writing a boring book report. Teachers may feel they have little time in the day to focus on children's social lives, and yet from the child's perspective, those bonds (or lack of them) come before anything else. Attending to a child's social well-being can be the key to helping her thrive in school.

Attending to a child's social well-being can be the key to helping her thrive in school.

Ms. Guthrie kept notes on Grace. Throughout each day for a week, she jotted down whom Grace talked to and who talked to Grace. She kept a note of whether Grace had a few real buddies or just randomly sat next to other kids during free time. She also looked for signs that Grace squabbled, as friends do. She eavesdropped, trying to get a feel for what Grace talked about when she was with others.

Ms. Guthrie realized that Grace was friendly to many of the children, and they to her. When the kids lined up, Grace often chatted with the girl in front of her. But when she listened to the actual conversations, she noticed that Grace's vocabulary was far bigger than the other children's. And she often popped out with fairly grown-up judgments about other kids' behavior. She sounded a little bossy, a little of what Ms. Guthrie's own mother would call schoolmarmish. When the children settled in for reading group, Grace listened to the others, and they to her. But her observations about the book were often a little too subtle or sophisticated for the rest of the group, even though it was the highest one. On the other hand, Ms. Guthrie heard no snickering and saw no mean glances behind Grace's back. Yet Grace never left the table arm in arm with one of the other girls. And any time there wasn't a structured lesson, Grace lingered near an adult.

Ms. Guthrie called Nina on the phone. She said, "I've been paying attention. Kids are not mean to Grace. And she is friendly toward the other kids in the room. She laughs at their jokes, she smiles when our class clown is entertaining everyone with his antics, and she is a super work partner. She notices when other kids are struggling with their work. And she's so bright, she often can help them. But I can see what worried you. She doesn't really have any best buddies."

Nina said in a tight and anxious voice, "Why not?"

Ms. Guthrie gave one of the best answers a teacher can offer. "I don't really know. I think I need to do a little more observation. I will call you one week from now and let you know what I've learned." To herself, Ms. Guthrie worried that it wasn't simply that Grace didn't really have any good friends. Maybe it was worse than that. Was she being left out in some way?

During the past two decades teachers have been flooded with information about how and why social relationships can go awry. In several high-profile cases, children who felt persecuted by peers have committed suicide, giving the issue added urgency. These cases have illuminated a dark side to the social lives of young children—the pain they can cause one another. Many children feel so distraught about a friendship gone awry that it blocks out everything else about their school experience. A kid who struggles at math or finds English class boring may still love school. A kid who has problems with friends finds it hard to pay any attention at all to classes. Once researchers turned their microscopes onto the pitfalls of children's friendships, they began investigating a problem that has, at one point or another, plagued every single classroom teacher: the loner (Asher and Wheeler 1985).

For most children, getting along with the larger group, as well as having a few good friends, seems as natural as drinking at the water fountain. In fact, for many children it's the best thing about school. Their favorite times of day are arrival, lunch, and recess. And many elementary school teachers accept the idea that while they toil over lesson plans and enticing activities that help children become readers or think about math, for many kids the most important part of the educational process is learning to navigate the social world. But as every teacher knows, making and keeping friends doesn't always go smoothly. And when it doesn't, it gets in the way of everything else. A child who is lonely often feels so sad and disconnected he is reluctant to come to school. Without friends, even the nicest school is not much fun, and the parts a child might otherwise excel in (reading, writing, or drawing, for instance) lose their appeal. Things are even worse for children who are actively teased or rejected. They may find it hard to concentrate on learning activities at all, distracted by the pain of exclusion. For the most part, when children leave at the end of the day, they are not thinking about long vowels or fractions. They are thinking about who sat next to them at lunch, whether they were chosen for a team at recess, and if they were invited to someone's birthday party. Though most teachers are aware of who is popular, who is left out, and which children hang out together, they typically see only the tip of the iceberg. It may be difficult for them to gather the information they'd need in order to know why a particular kid keeps annoying others or gets left out again and again.

Everyone knows a kid like this—either you were one, you knew one, or you've taught one. But in recent decades we've learned much more about the different reasons why a kid becomes a loner. Most teachers, after just a year or two in the classroom, can spot kids like that right away; they come into the room with a certain aura around them and a sad or blank look on their faces. They often end up in a seat away from others, eat lunch on their own, and are left standing solo when everyone is asked to pair up for an activity. During recess, such a child might linger on the edges of the playground. But those kids can also be identified by paying attention to what the other children are doing or not doing. They tend to avoid a loner, rarely making overtures or inviting such a child into a group activity. Sometimes it's worse than that. They actively dislike that child, pushing her away when she makes any attempt to join a cluster of kids.

Children who are ignored or rejected in one situation tend to experience the same painful thing in one setting after another, year after year. If the teacher in the toddler room identifies a child who annoys others, who constantly sparks conflicts, or who just never seems to find a buddy, the chances are when that same child is in preschool or third grade his teacher will notice the same problems. While researchers don't know *why* some children are plagued by these social deficits, they do know what kinds of behaviors are most problematic.

Most teachers know what it looks like: the child who keeps saying just the wrong thing to try to work his way into the cluster of kids playing a game. He taunts or boasts, instead of offering a good suggestion. He tries to boss the other kids, instead of quietly just joining in the game. She says things she thinks will impress the others, but just sounds to the others like she's boasting or saying things that are completely irrelevant. But what's going on inside his or her head, and why do some kids make the same social mistakes over and over again?

Children who are left out lack the ability to read the looks and words of others around them. They don't seem to pick up on the social cues that most of us use to tell us when we are connecting with people and when we are not. Children like this often fail to listen to the other children and don't seem to have the natural impulse to show interest in who the other child is or what he or she likes, doesn't like, and is good at or interested in. They interrupt, they talk through other kids, and they ignore the subtle cues about group dynamics. Again and again, they say or do just the wrong thing. They come wearing shin guards and soccer cleats, thinking it will impress the other kids who play on teams, but instead they elicit sarcasm and mirth. They brag about the cool toy they got the day before, thinking it will draw others to them, and instead come across as desperate or boastful. Some, hearing the easy banter between the other kids, try to come up with their own clever taunts and jokes, but instead sound aggressive and obnoxious. The child who always does and says the wrong thing, and is again and again left out by others, is at great risk for depression. Left untreated, the behaviors that contribute to a child's isolation continue, and so does the agony of being left out.

Research has shown that children like this are, unfortunately, fairly likely to have at least one parent who has similar difficulties. It may be that such deficits are inherited, but that really doesn't matter. The real problem, studies suggest, is that a parent who is unsociable doesn't create social opportunities outside of school for the lonely child; it's just not in his or her nature. And yet those opportunities are just what such a child needs, since activities with one or two peers outside of school give a child the chance to practice social interactions. It occurred to Ms. Guthrie that Nina's worry about Grace might stem from her own social isolation. But even if that were true, there was not much Ms. Guthrie could do about Nina's social quirks. Yet that didn't mean there was nothing she could do to try to tweak Grace's social skills. There are ways to help children who have difficulty making friends.

Friendship 101

Some studies have shown that children with social problems benefit enormously from short training programs. In one study, kids were put into groups of three; two of the children had been rated as popular by classmates, and one child was unpopular, based on sociometrics as well as teacher evaluations (Bierman and Furman 1984). Researchers told the triads that their help was needed in making videos to show university students what friends their age talked about and did together. They gave half of the groups coaching in three conversational skills: self-expression (sharing information about oneself and one's feelings), questioning (asking others about themselves and their feelings), and leadership bids (giving suggestions, advice, and invitations). They simply encouraged the other half to develop their ideas and work together. The unpopular kids who got the training improved their interactions even within the workgroup, eliciting better responses from the two popular kids with whom they were working. But just as significant, after the sessions were over, the unpopular kids in *all* the workgroups were more likely to make friends and earn higher marks on subsequent sociometrics. In other words, working with more popular kids helps children adjust the things they say and do. When they also get some direct instruction from grown-ups (dos and don'ts of friendship), they benefit even more.

In another training study, children who had social trouble participated in six weeks of after-school sessions in which they learned about friendships. Instructors taught them how to say nice things to a peer, ask other kids questions, show interest in what the other person said, and offer help in joint activities. After the sessions were over, those kids had better interactions in their classrooms (Asher and Hymel 1986).

But some research suggests that such elaborate training is not necessary. One of the problems ignored or disliked children face is that their awkward or unpleasant behavior prevents them from essential give-and-take with other kids that provides most children with lots and lots of practice at friendship. They do or say weird or abrasive things that distance them from other children, and the distance itself leads to more problems.

In one study, researchers asked children to go down a list of the other children in the class and indicate whom they most and least liked to play with. The researchers then reorganized the chairs so that each unpopular kid was seated next to several well-liked children. After six weeks, the unpopular children became better liked by all of the other kids in the class. In other words, one of the simplest ways to help disliked children become more popular is to subtly engineer the classroom so that they spend more time near the children who are liked. There are two reasons why this strategy works (Van den Berg and Cillessen 2015). First, it's a result of a sturdy and universal phenomenon: familiarity leads to liking. When people view a long series of images at a very high speed (too quickly to even identify the images) and are then asked to select the images they prefer, they always choose the ones that were flashed before them most frequently, even when they didn't know what they were seeing (Zajonc 1968). The pictures people were exposed to the most become the ones that are most liked. By the same token, being around someone more makes children like him or her more. Simply seating children next to one another makes them like one another. Perhaps once they feel greater affinity for the person, they are unconsciously motivated to justify that feeling by thinking of things they like about the person. The second reason is that by placing children who don't know how to be friends in proximity with better-liked ones, the unpopular children get chances to improve at making and keeping pals. Some simple changes can help disliked children become more liked. Those techniques, however, weren't going to help Ms. Guthrie; she had done enough careful observation to realize that Grace wasn't one of those children who are generally disliked.

Bullying: A Natural Behavior That Can Become a Problem

Meanwhile, as Ms. Guthrie calmly and methodically tried to get to the heart of the problem, Nina stayed awake at night feeling sad for Grace. Her sadness periodically lapsed into panic. She had heard from some other parents that there was a real bully in the third grade. Though the bully wasn't in Grace's classroom, maybe he was scaring Grace at recess or at the end of the school day. It wasn't an outrageous fear. In almost every school, there are one or two kids who are actual bullies (ironically, they are often chronically excluded themselves). These students are among the toughest for a teacher to deal with. They disrupt daily life for everyone. They need specific kinds of help, both in and out of the classroom. The problem of bullies is serious, but not pervasive. When Nina couldn't contain her new fear, she called Ms. Guthrie to find out if there was a bully in the third grade. Ms. Guthrie assured Nina that that was not the case. And as Nina replayed Grace's face on the way to and from school, she was comforted. Grace seemed to have a carefree swing to her gait, not that of a child worried that someone mean was about to torment her. But still, even if there wasn't some hateful child threatening Grace, maybe the other girls were deliberately ostracizing her. Nina knew all about that from her own childhood. Ms. Guthrie too, knew that people ganged up on one another and took pleasure out of choosing who was in and who was out of the group. All you had to do was sit around the teachers' lounge to see that there was an in-group of the cool teachers and there were those left out. Kids are just as good at this as grown-ups. And it's just as common.

Most kids lapse or leap into aggressive behavior now and then. Sometimes it sneaks up on the kids and the teacher. Here's a common example. A group of friends decides to form a club. It might start out with a perfectly reasonable focus: the kids form a band, work on a fort in the playground, or create a Lego club. Sometimes the activity is much more engaging to the members than the club itself. Members seem to flow in and out, and what really matters is building forts, collecting bugs, or enacting rock 'n' roll performances. But sometimes being part of the club is what really captures the attention of the members, providing them with a metaphorical umbrella for their time together. Clubs like these often don't start out as a way to exclude anyone. In fact, organizing themselves with a name and a purported identity is a perfectly natural pastime for children; it's one of the many ways they practice how to form, participate in, and govern groups. But, needless to say, like many components of childhood, there is the potential for trouble. At some point, clubs like these can take a wrong turn. Perhaps a child who is disliked by one of the members tries to join, and the group becomes preoccupied and energized by leaving that child out, rather than playing with Legos or building a fort. Suddenly, a benign and typical phenomenon becomes a vehicle for hurting other people's feelings.

There are also times when children form a club with the express intention of leaving out one or more kids. The clubs are somewhat mean to begin with. Children often feud with one another (again, a perfectly natural part of learning the dynamics of life in a community), and before you know it, some of the children have organized themselves into a group defined by a conflict with another child—the Mortal Enemy Club, the Pretty Girl Club, or the No Mikey Club (all of these were actual clubs formed at some point by children in excellent second- through fifth-grade classrooms). Establishing clubs like those reflects a natural impulse. But how teachers should best handle such an impulse is another question. Just because a behavior is normal doesn't mean it should be tolerated.

People tend to think that if a behavior is natural, it must be good. Paradoxically most people tend to also believe that if a behavior hurts others, it must signal a serious problem. Both beliefs are wrong. Exclusion is natural, but not that good. At the same time, wanting to leave others out or hurt them doesn't signal deviance. It's human to get angry, to want to hurt others, and to leave people out. Just as Nelson Mandela said, no one is born hating others because of the color of their skin or where they come from. But by the time children are old enough to make friends, they are also old enough to feel many of the impulses and emotions that go along with making friends—a desire to emulate, align, exclude, dominate, and influence. They aren't born hating others, but they are born with a strong drive to assert themselves, get what they need, and in many cases dominate. These feelings aren't pretty, but they're normal, and they serve important psychological functions. It would be impossible to grow up and survive in our complex and hierarchical society without learning, early on, how to operate with others, form alliances, and identify outsiders.

> *If a child grows up in a community (including school) where every activity has a winner and a loser, that is how they will set up situations themselves. If, on the other hand, they are put in situations that require cooperation, they are much more likely to develop skills for collaborating with others, and tolerating—or better yet, embracing—differences between people.*

But how children manage these subtle processes is shaped by what they see the adults around them doing. Just as importantly, however, it is shaped by the ways in which adults structure situations. If a child grows up in a community (including school) where every activity has a winner and a loser, that is how they will set up situations themselves. If, on the other hand, they are put in situations that require cooperation, they are much more likely to develop skills for collaborating with others and tolerating—or better yet, embracing—differences between people.

Classrooms That Foster Kindness

One well-known example comes from the work of the social psychologist Elliot Aronson. In 1959 the United States Supreme Court decided, in the case of *Brown v. Board of Education of Topeka*, that racial segregation in schools was unconstitutional. Many educators and psychologists (not to mention families) rejoiced, thinking that by bringing together children of different racial groups and from different backgrounds would reduce racial conflict and prejudice. However, in many places, teachers quickly found out that change didn't come that quickly. In fact, in places like Texas with large populations of new immigrants, Latinx children, who might or might not speak English at home, suffered even more when they were placed in classrooms with white or middle-class children. Hostilities were stronger than ever, and children from minority backgrounds found themselves even more uncertain of their academic potential and their place in school.

Aronson, who was then teaching at the University of Texas–Austin, was invited to come with his researchers to observe the classrooms and make some suggestions about what the administrators could do to make things better. But he arrived to observe with a strong theoretical framework: the power of cognitive dissonance. The theory goes like this: People like to feel that their thoughts and behaviors are consistent. When someone has two thoughts that are inconsistent with one another, or does something that is in conflict with a closely held belief, he feels discomfort (dissonance) and is unconsciously motivated to reduce that dissonance. In one famous example, experimental subjects were given a boring task (for example, sorting pennies or screwing caps on jars). Some of those subjects were paid, and some were not. After the job was over they were asked how they felt about the work. Intuitively, being paid for boring work should make it more appealing; after all, at least there's a financial reward. But in fact, people who weren't paid had better things to say about the menial dreary work ("It's good exercise for my hands," "It gives me time to think," "It's calming"). This is just what dissonance theory would predict. People tend to hold the belief that they are smart and capable; it creates dissonance to do stupid work for no pay. Motivated to reduce that dissonance, they come up with a rationale for why smart people such as themselves would do such stupid work with no reward.

When Aronson and his colleagues watched kids in the Texas schools stay separate, and saw white children exclude brown and black children from their play, workgroups, and lunch tables, he realized dissonance theory could help. He suggested that the teachers try putting children from different racial groups and backgrounds into small groups to work on assignments together. But that wasn't enough. For Aronson's plan to work, the students would have to really depend on one another. His thinking went like this: as long as white children could maintain their distance, they could continue to look down on children of color, but if their own academic success depended on some of those same children, dissonance would kick in. ("How could a smart kid like me need the help of that kid, if he's so dumb or bad? If I need his help, he must be smart and good.") Using his guidance, teachers in those schools put together workgroups made up of children who wouldn't ordinarily affiliate with one another. Within each workgroup, they gave every child a particular part of the material to learn. Then the children were supposed to teach one another the part each had learned. In that way, they couldn't do well on the test unless they all helped each other. Sure enough, after just six weeks of participating in these jigsaw classrooms, children exhibited much less interracial conflict, Latinx and black children felt better about themselves as students and liked school better, and white children reported liking and admiring children of color more (Aronson 1997). But the lesson of jigsaw extends to other conflicts besides racial ones. It's another example of how children's thoughts and behaviors often change the most not because they are punished for bad behaviors, or admonished, but because something about the structure of their experience subtly nudges them toward an internal change in perspective. There are other simple things teachers can do to nudge children toward collaboration.

The early childhood educator Vivian Gussin Paley came up with her own startlingly powerful yet simple way to restructure children's interactions (2009). Paley had noticed over the years that children often hurt one another's feelings by leaving them out of a game and that often being left out, or being the excluder, took on a life of its own, contributing to some of the worst dynamics in the room. Her classroom revolved around play, which she saw as the key to young children's intellectual and social development. So one year she decided to institute a very simple rule. Her students, as always, would have lots of opportunity and encouragement to play and freedom to take that play in many directions for long periods of time. But, they couldn't tell another child he or she could not join the play. It was not always easy to keep them to this rule. But it became easier over time. And by the end of the year, she found that not only were they adept at incorporating new participants (whether in the block corner, the dress-up corner, or the sandbox), but they were more inclusive and kinder during other parts of the day as well. She didn't lecture the children and she didn't punish them. She simply made inclusion a basic requirement of her classroom.

When children are hurtful to one another, they benefit from adult intervention. It's not just that adults can protect the hurt child, but more importantly, that all the children, the ones who have been mean and the ones who have been hurt, need to acquire ever more thoughtful and kind ways of interacting with one another.

Luckily there are many ways to mold and influence children's social behavior. Some of these are surprisingly subtle. One of the most obvious and powerful means by which children learn is simply from watching the way adults around them behave with one another. A vast body of research has shown that children emulate the grown-ups with whom they spend time. The more attached they are to those grown-ups, the more likely they are to imitate. We've long known that children who see and hear adults fight, yell, or hurt one another at home are much more likely to fight, yell, and hurt others when they are in school and beyond. It shouldn't be surprising that a similar dynamic occurs in school. After all, young children spend at least six hours a day, 180 days a year, with their teacher. If children see their teacher yelling (at other children or at one another), criticizing, teasing, or excluding, they are likely to do the same. Researchers think there are three routes by which children become more aggressive by observing aggression in the adults around them: they learn scripts for aggressive behavior (what to say and do when you want to hurt or dominate another person), they acquire ideas and thoughts that justify aggression (it's OK to be mean if the other person is annoying), and they experience feelings that make them want to be aggressive themselves.

Nor do children emulate only bad behavior. They also notice and imitate kind, supportive, and understanding behavior. Studies have shown that the language adults use to talk about feelings has a profound influence on children. Children who spend the first few years of life with parents who identify emotions by name

When children are hurtful to one another, they benefit from adult intervention. It's not just that adults can protect the hurt child, but more importantly, that all the children, the ones who have been mean and the ones who have been hurt, need to acquire ever more thoughtful and kind ways of interacting with one another.

and discuss people's feelings are more understanding and tolerant of other people's feelings when they are six. But naming feelings is just one step. Toddlers whose mothers refer to other people's mental states (what they are thinking about) grow up to have a much fuller understanding and acceptance of other people's emotions. Psychologists believe this is because understanding something about the thoughts of someone else who is angry or sad helps a child sympathize and tolerate the strong emotions of their peers. An intriguing set of studies shows that by the time children are in elementary school, the way they negotiate play and share toys varies from one culture to another. In one study researchers brought children into a play room, four at a time, gave them a really interesting and attractive new toy, and left them to figure things out on their own (French et al. 2011). Researchers were interested in how the children would share (or not share) the toy. But there was one more important feature to the study. Some of the children who were tested lived in China, and some lived in Canada. The recordings of their play showed that Chinese children were more assertive but also engaged in more spontaneous giving to one another. Canadian children, on the other hand, were more likely to mention common rules of sharing ("We should take turns"). In other words, by the time children are in school, their collaborations and their conflicts bear the fingerprint of society.

Watching and listening is only one way children learn how to get along, resolve conflict, exclude, include, and compromise. Engaging in chitchat is another. Children overhear a great number of stories about how people treat one another, from their parents, their teachers, their neighbors, and one another. Such stories convey a huge amount of information about what is acceptable and what is not in their community. Sometimes adults tell stories as a deliberate way to pass along some wisdom to children. But more often children overhear adults gossiping and soon begin gossiping with one another. They learn a lot from such gossip—not only what happened to various neighbors and family members but what people should or shouldn't have done, what's OK, what's not, what gets attention, what doesn't, and so forth. Everything we know about social learning theory suggests that children model a great deal of their own social behavior not only on the direct examples around them but also on what they hear about the lives of others.

When they are as young as five children gossip as a way to explore social norms. Often the informal conversations children have with one another, as well as the ones they have with grown-ups, or overhear grown-ups having with each other, are a powerful tool for shaping their ideas about social interactions.

Quirky Social Lives

Nina's worries about Grace had prodded Ms. Guthrie into a deep dive into the social complexities of eight- and nine-year-olds. Though she had, at this point, such a natural feel for the highs and lows of social dynamics in her classroom, that deep dive had helped her to take stock of what might be going on under the surface. But all of that general knowledge was just a backdrop, into which she wanted to place the particulars about Grace. She watched carefully to see if other children were mean to Grace. They weren't. They smiled at her. They chatted with her when she was standing in line. They listened when she said something during group meeting. It's true that the girls in her class were mean to one another some of the time. And their meanness was subtle. Ms. Guthrie had to really eavesdrop, and watch when the kids were at their most relaxed, to get a feel for some of the darker social dynamics. One little girl named Alison seemed like the queen bee. She had three friends who congregated around her whenever they could. Sometimes Alison would look over at another kid and then begin talking to her buddies with an authoritative tone and a conspiratorial look on her face. Ms. Guthrie was pretty sure at those moments Alison was telling her friends that another child smelled bad, had stupid shoes, or didn't even know the national anthem. She heard Alison announce to another girl that she hadn't made it onto the soccer team. Ms. Guthrie assured the little girl that the soccer team hadn't been formed yet. But generally Ms. Guthrie tended to stay out of those exchanges. She thought kids had to work some of this out on their own. She trusted that by and large most of them were pretty resilient. And besides, she couldn't micromanage every exchange. Meanwhile, she had no sense that the other girls were spreading mean tales about Grace. It seemed to Ms. Guthrie that Grace never gave them the chance. Yet Grace seemed so eager to be friends with her and with the librarian. She was very easy in her exchanges with adults; she had a big vocabulary and a genuine interest in the lives of grown-ups. That in itself made her stand out. Some of the children in the class acted as if grown-ups didn't even exist. Ms. Guthrie wondered if she should pay more attention to Grace's love of adults.

Years before, when Ms. Guthrie had had small children, she'd had a good friend named Jen who used to come visit with her own small children. Usually about five mothers would get together one afternoon a week for coffee while the kids played. But Jen's little girl Iris, who was three, never joined the pack. She'd wander into the kitchen, where the moms were talking, and linger. Once Ms. Guthrie's own daughter

Janie had invited Iris to her fourth birthday party. When Iris arrived, the other kids were outside decorating cupcakes and playing with Hula-Hoops. Iris barely glanced at them, instead heading straight into the kitchen, where Ms. Guthrie was assembling the rest of the party fare. Iris looked around somewhat baffled, saying to Ms. Guthrie with a confused frown on her forehead, "Where are all the ladies?" She had found her people and wanted them. Those other people, her size, held little appeal for her.

There was one remaining thing Ms. Guthrie wanted to do before meeting again with Nina. She wanted to talk with Grace. Not for sixty seconds when Grace handed in her collage or a few minutes while the children ate snack. She wanted to have a real conversation. She invited Grace to eat lunch with her on Friday. She brought cookies to make it special. The other kids went to the cafeteria, and Grace happily stayed behind. They sat at one of the kids' tables and chatted about all kinds of things—their favorite books, where Ms. Guthrie went in the summertime, and how much they both loved to eat chocolate. Finally Ms. Guthrie asked Grace who her best friends were in the class. Grace shrugged. "I dunno. I don't really have one best friend. I don't know why everyone talks about a best friend all the time. I mean, I like Rosa and Meg. They're smart and funny. But you know, sometimes they're awfully silly and I just want to tell them to simmer down." Grace had that slightly haughty look on her face, which Ms. Guthrie imagined must put off the other kids. Then Grace added with a warm, eager look on her face, "Who is your best friend, Ms. Guthrie?"

Ms. Guthrie was taken aback. Wasn't this her time to find out about Grace? Then she reminded herself that you can't elicit information from children if you don't offer a little. "Well, my sister is my best friend, really. She lives over a thousand miles away, but we talk almost every day on the phone."

"Yeah, right," said Grace enthusiastically. "Me too. My family, my mom, is my best friend." As the conversation unfolded, Ms. Guthrie felt reassured.

There's nothing intrinsically wrong with liking the company of people in a different age group. One of the worst misuses of our increased knowledge about how children change with age is to rush to the conclusion that because a child of a certain age is somewhat different from other children of that age, something must be wrong with her or him. Milestones can be very valuable in reassuring parents and teachers, and failure to reach some milestones is, some of the time, a red flag for other problems. But sometimes different is just different. Why should children of five or eight be less distinctive and quirky than we adults? Our age doesn't define us, and neither does theirs. Grace had a bigger vocabulary than most children her age. She loved books, and through books had not only learned about people of other ages but come to feel that she *knew* them. After all, that is one of the documented values of reading fiction: it expands your social and psychological landscape. Grace, who lived alone with her mom, relished the way in which all the stories she read filled her home life with people and events from other places and times. She spent a great deal of time with her mother, and that, too, gave her ease with adults.

As Ms. Guthrie took stock of all the information she had gathered, she felt that this was just who Grace was. For now, she liked to separate herself a little from the other kids. She liked to talk to other people who read the way she did—that meant grown-ups. She liked to analyze people's behavior. Other kids weren't so into that. Teachers, on the other hand, were like her. They liked to chat with her. They laughed at her subtle jokes and probed her unusual ideas. They were calm and reasonable and friendly. She liked studying the ways of grown-ups—their phrases and their mannerisms.

Ms. Guthrie had the feeling that Grace watched the other girls fume, whisper, and laugh. She wasn't oblivious. Just not eager to jump into the fray. She might need more time to figure out who she was, in relation to the others. There was nothing wrong with that. Over the years Ms. Guthrie had come to feel that the child whose academic skills, friendships, and pastimes were all on an even keel was the exception, not the rule. Maybe Grace's avid reading, huge vocabulary, and interest in information had come first, and a lively social life would come a little later.

Ms. Guthrie encouraged Nina to step back a bit. She promised she would touch base with her in February and tell her if her view had changed. But by late January, Grace was eating lunch with a small group of girls, deep in the middle of conversation with three or four others, every single day. Yet Grace was still Grace, and children don't change all at once. She still went to the library for recess.

CHAPTER FOUR

Harry's Math Problem

———— ◆ ————

Play ★ Learning ★ Cognition: Part Two ★
Learning How to Learn

IT WASN'T UNTIL November that Luke first really zeroed in on Harry. The year had gotten off to a good start. Luke had a feisty group, just the way he liked it. As always, he played the guitar for the kids each morning, and they immediately took to his energetic, breezy style. He had quickly pegged the two kids who were going to need the most help academically. He also knew, by the end of the first week, that he'd have to keep a close eye on a little boy named Peter; he already had said rude, angry things to several other children without any provocation. Luke had a pretty good sense that one particular cluster of girls would form the social core of his classroom that year, for better or for worse. He had even figured out which girl was at the center of that cluster. And, as he had admitted ruefully to his wife, he felt especially tuned in to the boys in his room. He could still easily remember what it was like to be in fifth grade, and because he had grown up with three brothers, he really felt he got the boy thing.

Luke found it easy to sort fifth-grade boys into various bins. There are the ones who can sit still and focus and the ones who cannot. The ones who seem confident and bouncy (often they are also the ones who are athletic) and the ones who hang back, or worse, tease and bully because they feel excluded. But that quick sorting could only take Luke so far. Beginning his fourth year of teaching, he was savvy enough to realize that there was more to every child than one or two bins. Harry was going to be more of a puzzle than Luke had thought.

Harry had dark red hair, which lay on his scalp in thick curls, like a knit cap. He had lean limbs and seemed to have amazing muscle tone already, though he was nowhere near puberty. Luke himself had been an athlete in high school, and he could see from the way Harry moved around the room that he too would shine in high school sports. He had an aura that Luke had seen before and experienced from the inside out. It attracted other kids to him. Before Harry had even put away his lunch box, two or three other boys had drifted over to his side, where they began talking in exuberant voices, laughing and gesticulating.

Nor was his ease and confidence just for joking around and recess. When the class gathered to discuss a story, Harry would almost always raise his hand and contribute a thought or reaction. He said interesting things, and he said them in an economical and clear way. His comments were specific; he read the books and re-membered what he had read. He had a great vocabulary. Luke hadn't yet asked for much real writing, but on the few assignments he had given, Harry answered well, if briefly. Luke mentally checked the boxes for smart and good reader. It would be easy to help Harry strengthen his writing and reading—just give him great books to read, offer specific feedback, and begin to get him in the habit of making each sentence just a little clearer and more vivid. He might try to encourage Harry to expand a little more on each idea. He was ready to discover the power of revision. Those all seemed like just the right tasks for a bright fifth grader.

When Luke stood back and watched the group working, as he liked to do now and then, he noticed that even though Harry was so gregarious, he often spent his free time alone at the workbench, which Luke had set up against one wall. Harry seemed magnetically drawn to making various contraptions (cars, airplanes, boats, tiny furniture, nunchucks, and other gadgets) with whatever bits of wood, nails, and metal were lying in the colored plastic containers at the back of the workbench. He seemed equally absorbed by taking apart all kinds of small machines, which Luke collected and brought in for just this purpose. Whenever something broke or wasn't working correctly in the classroom (the pencil sharpener, a broken scooter from the playground, the class microscope), Harry eagerly volunteered to fix it. Harry could be bumptious and impulsive at times (the kind of kid who couldn't resist any ball he saw lying on the ground, compelled to aim it toward a trash can, bounce it off the top of the door, or toss it to a friend). But not when he was at the workbench. There, other people and activities disappeared, and he became completely focused, his large hands comfortably manipulating small pieces and delicate tools, as he worked on whatever small project had drawn him in. All of the ways in which Harry seemed confident, competent, and engaged must have been why Luke was so surprised when he stumbled upon Harry's Achilles' heel.

When it came to math, Harry didn't seem confident or engaged. It wasn't that he appeared obviously confused. He didn't complain when it was math period. He wasn't one bit disruptive while doing math work. He didn't ask for help. He handed in his homework on time. There was nothing bold to catch Luke's attention. Harry didn't get all of the problems right on the weekly quizzes they took to help Luke track how his students were doing, but Luke didn't expect that from any of the students. Harry got enough of them correct, enough of the time, to make Luke explain away his mediocre quiz results. Perhaps he wasn't that great at tests. Maybe it was just that a fair amount of the material was new to him. Perhaps he was busy trying to understand the newly introduced concepts and focused on getting quicker and more accurate in his mental calculations. The truth is, Luke didn't think much at all about those scores during the first few months of the year. They didn't fit with his overall sense of Harry, and so he shrugged them off as being insignificant.

But then in November all of the students took a standardized test, which the teachers in his school used to measure their students' grasp of the fifth-grade math curriculum. Luke didn't love the test, but it wasn't terrible either. It gave teachers, in broad strokes, a good sense of who needed far more challenging work, who seemed to be mastering a reasonable amount of the new concepts and strategies, and who might be headed for academic trouble. To Luke's surprise, Harry was one of those kids. His scores were down in the bottom of the bottom quartile. Luke felt a little panicked. Harry hadn't been getting the math at all. It didn't make sense.

Harry was so obviously smart. But it wasn't only his overall intelligence that seemed at odds with his math score. He was so particularly drawn to all things mechanical. Now that Luke thought about it, it seemed to him that Harry was made for math. So why was he struggling so? And if he had been having trouble all fall, how come he had never asked for help? What was going on? What had he missed?

Luke had come face-to-face with one of the biggest conundrums in education. Why is it that a child can appear to have such a natural feel for words, numbers, or shapes in his everyday life and yet struggle so to master the academic version of those skills? Why would a bright child who was naturally drawn to all things involving shapes, measurement, and spatial arrangements, a child who had enough skill in reading and could keep score in a game like nobody's business, be doing so badly in math? What was the difference between the kinds of natural math Harry was so good at, and the kinds of math that filled the workbook and the test? The answer begins with a close look at what children do long before they encounter things like math problems and workbooks: they play.

Play: The Foundation of Academics

If you think about it, children first encounter nearly everything they are supposed to learn at school long before they get there. They begin discovering the principles that govern the natural world by stacking blocks, divvying up toys, building space-ships, mixing potions, and so on. They count, measure, estimate, and predict every single day whenever they clean up their toys, eat cookies, set the table, and watch to see what the bug will do after they pull off its wing. Daily life holds endless opportunities for the growing mind to expand.

If you think about it, children first encounter nearly everything they are supposed to learn at school long before they get there.

Even something that seems as strictly academic as algebra makes its first appearance in early childhood. Long before middle schoolers learn the order of operations, or ninth graders solve for x, five-year-olds begin trying to figure out things like how many nickels they'll need to buy five seven-cent pieces of bubble gum at the corner store or how many more small red building blocks they'll need to make the right wing of an airplane balance the big blue ones used on the left wing.

The same can be said of the skills children will tackle in science, language arts, and social studies. Children encounter nearly all the core components of each of the foundational academic disciplines in their everyday lives, doing what comes naturally to them. This might include chores like setting the table, family routines like raking leaves and planning outings, and daily errands like grocery shopping. (Though to some extent, children benefit from daily routines only when they live in families with some degree of order and adult involvement. If your father never explains to you why he's buying the big box of cereal instead of the small box, or your family life is too chaotic for chores and rituals, you won't learn as much in these home settings.) But the activity that pervades nearly all children's lives and comes *most* naturally to them is play. And, as researchers have so amply demonstrated, play affords the richest possible avenue for intellectual work (Fisher et al. 2011).

Work and Play Reversed

Ordinarily, teachers and parents sort children's activities into two categories: work and play. When children amuse themselves, make up games, tell stories, interact with other children, and initiate their own activity, it's considered play. Work is whatever a child does that someone else insists on (cleaning up their room, helping out with household chores, and most importantly, school). Even within school, we segregate the purposeful, goal-oriented activity that leads to academic gains from the other parts of the day. Recess is the short time in the school schedule when children are allowed to take a break from their "work" in order to play. We let them play before and after but not during lessons. However, this set of labels for categorizing children's activities, though seemingly innocuous, leads to a serious misunderstanding of cognitive development. To understand why this is so important, it's worth examining why we think a given activity is or is not play.

Counter to what most people think, it's not *what* children do, the materials they use, or even their mood that renders their activity play. We tend to think that if children are using toys, or laughing, or playing a recognized game, it must be play, and that when they are doing chores or learning school material, it must be work. Play might involve a game like traffic jam or chess, pretending to be doctors, or throwing a ball. But play might just as easily involve hammering nails, planning an imaginary trip with another child, laboriously digging a hole in the dirt, or even cleaning the tables. Children's play can occur in the car, in the grocery line, while doing math, or in circle time. They might look delighted or joyful, but they might also look dead serious, or even distraught. Play is not a certain activity, nor is it the opposite of work. Not in childhood. Play is a psychological stance toward the world.

> *Play is not a certain activity, nor is it the opposite of work. Not in childhood. Play is a psychological stance towards the world.*

Two characteristics distinguish play from nonplay in childhood. The first defining characteristic of play is that the activity is intrinsically meaningful to the child.

When children are playing they do it not for a promised prize or because someone has told them they must, but because they want to. It might be joyous, but oftentimes when children play they encounter frustration, hurt feelings, or disappointment. What's so striking is that feeling bad rarely keeps a child from continuing her play. Take, for instance, the child whose block structure keeps collapsing because it does not have a wide enough base or is too tall. When it falls, she might cry. But she's likely to build it again. Similarly, when two children fight over who gets to be the mommy in a make-believe scenario, they might get angry at one another. But they're unlikely to give up their game of house. They keep at it because it is so satisfying and meaningful to them.

The second defining characteristic of children's play is that the activity, whether it involves make-believe, construction, competitive games with rules, or more open-ended exploration, does not have real-world consequences. In other words, within the framework of play, a child might enact a battle, marry, create an army, or build a tower. But the child never for one moment thinks her activity will have real-life consequences. This "as if" stance is the invisible framework that renders any activity play and distinguishes it from all nonplay. When children take the "as if" stance, they can consider and try endless permutations, experiments, and speculations about themselves and the world. Just consider a few examples. Imagine two children enacting a superhero fight; they might try it one way and then decide that the next time, the superhero can fly rather than run. They might decide that a third time, the bad guy will punch the good guy. In other words, they try alternative versions of a scenario. Or, imagine two children are making paper airplanes. They fold the paper and send it. It drops. They decide they want to make it fly farther, so they add something to the wings. They fly it and it crashes to the ground. They have a new idea; they'll fold it so the nose is longer and thinner. They keep at it for an hour, each time speculating about what will make it work, taking stock of their successes and failures, and going from there. And children often take this "as if" stance while doing more prosaic activities. Watch a child who is supposed to be cleaning out the jars of paint at the sink become absorbed by what happens when he mixes the colors and then controls the way the mixed color drops onto the sink bottom. He can stick with this absorbing exploration for longer than it would take to actually just clean the jar and get far more out of it than he might a lesson in the properties of liquids. The opportunity to think and rethink is a huge part of why play is such an essential activity for intellectual development.

What are the specific benefits of play? Researchers have shown that when children envision a dramatic scenario in their play, plan a Lego building, or argue over the rules of a new game, they practice what's referred to as counterfactual thinking (Harris 2000). They learn to speculate about alternative outcomes in the future and in the past. They will need that skill in order to think through decisions of all kinds (political, medical, financial, and personal). The same powerful cognitive process is also essential for the kinds of academic analysis required in history, math, and science classes. But children also learn to communicate, invent, find different solutions to the same problem, break an activity up into its components, and think from someone else's perspective. Nor are the benefits only cognitive and academic. As they play, children also learn to negotiate, collaborate, and compromise. Moreover, children acquire these skills across a wide range of kinds of play, whether it's when they are making up silly sentences with the words on their spelling sheets, deep into a drama in the dress-up corner, inventing a new machine with scraps from old equipment, having fun at the lunch table, digging in the sand, or just making up jokes and stories while standing in line.

Finally, because, by definition, the value of play comes from the fact that the child wants to play, and has to come up with the play him- or herself, any attempt to simply make a lesson playful misses the very psychological characteristic that renders play such a powerful means for learning during childhood. Play is the child's work.

The benefits of such play cannot simply be isolated and infused into more conventional academic activities. It can be tempting for teachers to try to make activities that are nothing like play (practicing addition facts, defining words, making up sentences, or writing book reports) more appealing by inviting children to decorate the page; choosing content or examples that seem silly or lively (posing math problems that involve ice cream or soccer matches); or adding a competitive gamelike quality (practicing addition facts by getting kids to try to finish by the time a bell rings and then giving them a prize). These small flourishes might make certain dreary tasks more fun, but they won't transform a nonplay activity into play. There are three reasons why. First, children throw themselves into the intellectual and social challenges presented by building forts, enacting superheroes and animals, digging tunnels, and inventing games because they so desperately want to engage in the play itself. They are willing to forge their way through any number of puzzles, setbacks, and conflicts, and have enormous energy and stamina for such activity. The commitment and industriousness elicited during their own spontaneous play cannot easily be simulated in activities imposed by an adult, no matter how delightful the activities may seem to the adult suggesting them. Second, most of the time children's play is quite complex. Usually, even a five-minute stretch draws on several kinds of psychological processes: a child at play may need to invent new uses for available objects; use his imagination to transform objects and settings; recall specific roles he wants to reenact (doctors, firefighters, and parents, to name just a few); borrow conventional tropes and rules from songs, stories, and everyday scenarios he has witnessed; and negotiate a variety of information, interpretations, and plans with his playmates. For the most part, children's own spontaneous play is bound to be more intellectually challenging to them than any playlike activity a teacher imposes. The intellectual benefits cannot be predetermined. If and when adults try to co-opt play in this way, the underlying structure and value of play are quickly undermined. Finally, because, by definition, the value of play comes from the fact that the child *wants* to play, and has to come up with the play him- or herself, any attempt to simply make a lesson playful misses the very psychological characteristic that renders play such a powerful means for learning during childhood. Play *is* the child's work.

Harry offered a perfect example of what scientists have learned about play. Left to his own devices, he had honed many mathematical (as well as scientific and literary) skills while playing. Through his contraptions, his tinkering, and his problem solving at the workbench, he had stretched himself intellectually and practiced key mental tools for higher-order thinking. He could do math when it was part of one of his projects. But by fifth grade, he still hadn't figured out how to parlay that into the kind of math he encountered in the workbook and on the test; nor had he encountered teachers who had helped him make this transfer.

Implicit Versus Explicit Learning

Harry presented a puzzle that developmental psychologists have been circling around for years: the relationship between implicit and explicit learning. We know that children acquire an astounding amount of knowledge without knowing they are doing so—how to talk, navigate the social worlds of friends and family, organize the world into useful categories (animals, furniture, tools, vehicles, etc.), compute (given any semblance of everyday life, most children learn the fundamental premise of adding and subtracting), and the ability to test hypotheses, just to name a few. They also acquire vast stores of information; many children by four know a great deal about animals, trucks, the routes near their homes, characters in television shows, the rules of various games, and how to operate a smartphone, for instance. The ability to assimilate a huge amount of very complex material and use it appropriately each day tends to go virtually unnoticed most of the time, because it happens below the surface, with little deliberate effort on the part of the young learner or parents, siblings, or caregivers. This casual and nearly invisible process of learning is not a quirk nor a fleeting aspect of early childhood. It is the fundamental characteristic of early psychological development. Children learn all the time as a part and parcel of their everyday lives. Key to this somewhat seamless process is another equally distinct feature of early childhood: the world appears to young children with fewer boundaries than it does to older children and adults.

German developmental psychologist Heinz Werner (1948) argued that babies experience the world in an undifferentiated holistic way—a cry of hunger, the appearance of Mother's face, the act of nursing, and the feeling of satisfaction are all part of the same phenomenon. To the toddler, the colored blocks, the feelings they evoke, the impulse to stack them, and envisioning the tower she might build are also part of one big gestalt. Neither the baby nor the toddler separates the different aspects of any experience. Each experience and event is encountered as one undifferentiated blob. Development, Werner said, involves the gradual process of separating the elements of an experience into separate compartments: a word, the thing it names, the connotations of that thing, and its functions become more distinct from one another. For instance, a four-year-old knows that the word *ball* can be replaced by another word, and the object will still be what it is: a round thing that rolls and bounces. He can see a ball, and even think about what he might do with it, without actually touching it. This increasing categorization of experience into different levels and types (words, intentions, objects, events, goals, and people) forms the basis of a more abstract way of thinking. Children begin to understand that their thoughts and intentions are separate from the objects of those thoughts and intentions: a five-year-old knows that she can think about eating the chocolate bar without eating it, she can imagine it spread with peanut butter, can envision a scenario in which she hides it from someone else, and can even plan a drawing in which the chocolate bar is five feet tall. The new kind of differentiated thinking allows for a very important new academic skill—the ability to learn something outside of its natural context. A child can think about adding pizza slices without actually adding any. She can learn about places and people she hasn't directly encountered. She can think through situations without having to enact them. And increasingly, she can think about basic patterns and logical sequences that aren't tied to any particular content (the basis of all higher mathematics and logic). But that process of learning without direct instruction is gradual and cannot be forced or rushed. Even once children enter school, their cognitions emerge in the context of activities that are compelling and meaningful to them.

Children often do their best thinking when they aren't thinking about learning.

When Soviet psychologist Istomina asked five-year-olds to recall lists of words they had heard just a few moments before, they seemed completely unable to recall more than three or four words on the list (1975). Psychologists used to attribute such limited memory capacity to young children's "limited memory span." However, Istomina then set up a play grocery store in the room adjacent to the children's classroom. She gave the children play money and asked them to "go to the store" and "buy some groceries," listing the same number and kind of items that had been so difficult for them to remember in a more conventional memory task. In the play frame of playing store, they easily remembered as many as seven items. Istomina's study is just one classic example of research showing that young children think at a higher level when they are engaged in activities they find meaningful and engaging. It's worth noting that the children in Istomina's study were not trying to remember things in order to do well at school. They were trying to remember things in order to "shop." Children often do their best thinking when they aren't thinking about learning.

It turns out that even when children are learning more academic material, they continue to solve problems and devise intellectual strategies without realizing it (Siegler 1998). Researcher Robert Siegler asked ten-year-old children to solve math problems like the following: $5 + 7 - 5 = ?$ He was interested in how quickly they would identify the underlying rule that the first and third numbers cancel each other out. He could track exactly when children had discovered the rule by measuring how long it took them to solve a series of similar math problems; it takes longer to solve the problem by calculating it ($5 + 7 = 12$ and $12 - 5 = 7$) than by applying the rule. By timing the children as they worked on the problems, he learned that they began using the shortcut (which reduced the time it took them to find the answers) before they were able to say how they were doing it. In other words, children learn new things without realizing exactly what they are doing (Siegler also found that though the children used the rule without being aware of their process, they did eventually identify and articulate the rule they had devised). But as children get older, the implicit natural approach to learning is not enough.

Reflection: The Turbo Power

At some point, a little more distance and reflection becomes very powerful. Young children are not aware that they are learning, and they have little sense of how they go about learning. They are just totally *in it*. Yet by five or so, this changes. They begin to think about their own learning and their own thoughts, acquiring what psychologists call metacognition. In the first research of this sort, Ann Brown (1997) was interested in why six-year-olds are so much better at remembering than four-year-olds. She didn't accept the current wisdom that their memory span was simply increasing (as if memory span were like muscle length or vocal power—something that just grew over time). Instead, she argued, children of five and six were becoming aware of their own learning. As a result they began to be more deliberate in trying to remember things. They developed mnemonics and strategies for remembering. So, for instance, if you tell a four-year-old to remember someone's name, he'll nod at you and then not give it another thought until he is asked for the name. He might or might not remember (as every parent knows, toddlers and preschoolers can exhibit astonishing memory for particular things), but he'll have virtually no inclination or ability to try to remember something. He simply either will or won't. However, by the age of six, children will repeat something they want to remember out loud, tie a string on their finger, or come up with a rhyme as an aid to recalling. All of these reflect their new awareness that cognition is a specific mental process and that they can try to control it.

Metacognition is involved with far more than simple memory tasks. In a ground-breaking series of experiments, Brown extended her ideas about the value of asking children to reflect on their own learning. First she asked elementary school children to study various materials about animals in their environments as part of a science project. She reasoned that when children had to make sure another child learned what they now knew, the children would be forced to make their new knowledge explicit. In a second control group, children learned the same exact material, also in groups, as had the first. But instead of teaching it to others, they simply wrote a report or took a test on what they had learned. The children who taught the information to others learned the material far better than did those in the control group.

That kind of metacognition not only deepens a child's specific knowledge but also enables her to apply what she has learned to new domains. Learning to reflect on your own learning and lift skills from one context to another is so essential in our society that without it, children are at a huge disadvantage.

In the 1960s Sylvia Scribner became interested in how schooling affected the way children think. Her initial insight came on the heels of Arthur Jensen's inflammatory research, presented in the *Harvard Educational Review (1969)*, claiming to show that black children had poorer memories than white children. His research appeared to support the argument that there were intrinsic differences in intelligence between white and black children by showing that black children couldn't recall as many items on a list as white children could. Scribner, who had already done a great deal of research looking at the impact of formal schooling on the way people think, set out to show that in fact, most of the black children in Jensen's study had spent considerably less time in school than their white counterparts. She reasoned that by not going to school, they had missed out on important reading skills, which in turn had prevented them from acquiring certain conceptual or abstract ways of thinking. While white children who had gone to school were likely to organize the lists of words into abstract categories like fruit, tools, and clothing, the black children who had often missed weeks or months of school because of their living conditions instead simply relied on their memory spans, a far less effective strategy. Scribner and her colleagues redid Jensen's recall task, reading a list of items to children and then asking them to recall as many items on the list as they could. But, based on her hunch, she added a twist. She asked the children to recall the items from various categories (e.g., "Can you recall the fruits? How about all the items of clothing?"). When she gave the black children this one strategy (using conceptual categories to organize their memory), they did just as well as the white children had. It wasn't their intellectual capacities (or even just their memories) that were lacking. It was that they hadn't learned an explicit strategy for remembering long lists, a strategy that comes to most of us by way of schooling (Scribner 1986).

Scribner began to wonder about other ways in which decontextualized thinking might offer a benefit to students. She decided to compare two groups of teenagers: those who learned math in a conventional school setup (abstract problems, math sheets, etc.) and those who used similar math in their daily work but had no formal instruction in math outside of that context. For her study she chose subjects who all lived in a town with a huge dairy plant. The workers there were highly skilled at using complex algorithms to load each specific dairy order onto trays in the most efficient way possible. When it came to loading the trays, the dairy workers were far superior to the high school students, who struggled to identify and apply the mathematics necessary for loading the trays quickly and efficiently. Unsurprisingly, the high school students were far better at the paper-and-pencil number problems. Each group was better at the math tasks it was used to. However, Scribner's team then gave all of the young people (from the high school and the dairy plant) a new kind of math to learn, one neither group had ever encountered but that was an offshoot of the kind of math both groups had previously used, albeit in two very different ways. The high school students were much more able than the dairy workers to use what they already knew to learn something new. In other words, the explicit, isolated, more formal kind of learning required in school offers a powerful advantage over the kind of in-context implicit learning that happens in even the most highly skilled jobs.

To sum up, we know that children learn implicitly and that such implicit learning often underlies their fastest, most powerful intellectual accomplishments, particularly before and throughout elementary school. On the other hand, we also know that children become more able to explicate and monitor their learning as they get older and that such metacognition adds significant power to their educational experiences.

A Bridge for Harry

Luke began to rethink Harry's math problem. The contrast between implicit and explicit presented him with a new way of framing Harry's difficulty. He felt that it was important for children in his class to get better at learning how to learn—to figure out how a skill or piece of information they learned in one context could be extracted and applied to a new context. Clearly, Harry was using arithmetic and mathematical thinking every time he built a new, more intricate paper airplane, planned a new circuit for his small handmade gravity cars, or calculated the materials he'd need to build a new catapult. His trouble was not mathematical per se. He struggled over applying what he knew and could do, without even thinking about it, to the kinds of decontextualized problems presented in conventional schoolwork. Yet Luke knew that it would be important for Harry to eventually understand math in a more decontextualized and formal way. But, he realized, that was a gradual process, and the abstract reflective approach could grow out of the more concrete embedded approach. Harry wouldn't be able to distill what had seemed so natural when he was building things and transfer it to new situations if Luke didn't help him formalize his knowledge.

Luke decided that he would begin asking Harry, at least once a week, to explain to another student how he was calculating things for his projects. After a few weeks of this, he suggested that Harry create a set of activity cards that other kids could use to build the contraptions, toys, and gadgets he had built. Luke figured activities like this would lead Harry to put his intuitions into words and diagrams—a crucial step in making implicit knowledge explicit and concrete thinking more abstract. Luke hadn't waved a magic wand. But by coming up with activities that began with Harry's mathematical strengths and led him toward the aspects of math he found difficult, Luke had offered him a bridge.

By the time Harry got to sixth grade, the math that had seemed like a different language to him had turned into a familiar (albeit somewhat dry and less exciting) way of thinking. By taking stock of Harry's developmental past, Luke had found a way to build a path toward Harry's educational future.

CHAPTER FIVE

Sometimes It's Good to Tiptoe

———◆———

Attachment and Separation ★ Teacher-Student
Interactions ★ Parent-Child Interactions

MARGO STOOD UP in front of the group of elementary school teachers. Though she had retired several years before, she still thought of herself as a teacher. In fact, she continued to feel more comfortable talking to a group of fourth graders than a group of grown-ups.

Legendary in her district, she'd been asked by the principal to give a presentation during a professional development day. She felt a little nervous as she began: "Teaching has always been my passion and I never had any other career in mind since I was in kindergarten and was allowed to collect the milk money in a small milk carton with the top cut off. One of the reasons I loved this profession so much was due to the success I experienced forging relationships with the students in my class every year. That is, until PJ walked into my room on the first day of school, seven years ago."

Margo had taught for twenty-seven years, twenty-two of them in the same rural school district. She had been as beloved by the kids who struggled as she had been by the ones who excelled. She was warm, confident, and uncannily attuned to the ups and downs of fourth graders. She seemed to connect with tightly wound kids and dreamy kids, with the chatterboxes and the silent ones. She got along with the class leaders and the wallflowers, the athletes and the bookworms. Each kid felt he or she had a special link with Margo. Sometimes people think that the teachers who have an easy and warm rapport with students do not know how to bring out the best work in students, that somehow teachers are either warm *or* rigorous. As if one has to make a choice between being the loving teacher and the one who fires children up about academics. But Margo did both. She was a reader and a writer, and she got her kids to feel like readers and writers. She brought an amazing array of poetry, essays, and short stories into her classroom, to read aloud and to leave on the bookshelves for the children to read and use throughout the year. She had a wide frame of reference about history, art, and fiction.

It wasn't only that she got her students to love reading and writing. She also helped them get better at both. Year after year, boys and girls of all abilities wandered out of her room at recess and dismissal, chatting about their favorite books, discussing whether they preferred writing haiku or quatrains, and flinging themselves into heated debates about the meaning of a particular word. At the end of the year, her students had acquired larger vocabularies, were more able to form clear sentences, and were more likely to put their thoughts coherently onto paper.

But that was not all. She also seemed able, with her glowing smile and hushed, intense voice, to create an almost instant sense of order and authority in the classroom. She was gentle but kids knew she was in charge. Wildness was not permitted in her classroom. But, as she was about to tell the audience of teachers facing her, even equipped with such a formidable array of teaching strengths, she had an Achilles' heel. It was the same Achilles' heel every single good teacher has: the students.

No matter what skills and attributes a teacher is equipped with, all of the students come to class armed with their own array of quirks and forces, and those are just as formidable as the teacher's tools. Margo didn't usually let this worry her. Especially not in September. She started out each year eager to discover her students' idiosyncrasies—their demons and their gifts—on her own and in her own way. She explained to the teachers:

"Every June before the end of the school year, we went through a process of receiving our class lists, meeting with the previous teachers of our 'new' students, and going over any relevant IEPs. It was my custom to avoid obtaining too much information, especially the other teachers' stories. I did not want to be biased by others' opinions or struggles. I believed that too much information would only interfere with my ability to see my new students as they were presently with no negative impressions. So, when PJ walked into my classroom on that first day I had reviewed his IEP and knew a bit about him from his family name—living in a small community, a child's name could fortunately or unfortunately be its own label—but other than that vague reputation, and his IEP, I knew next to nothing.

"My first impression was that he was aloof. I had a sense that he was mature beyond his years. He didn't laugh easily or seem to have much interest in what was happening in our classroom that first week. It was my goal to accomplish two things at the beginning of the year. Number one, first and foremost, I wanted to form a bond with my students. It may be cliché, but one of my strongest beliefs is that kids don't care what you know until they know that you care. My second goal always was to build a strong community of learners. I wanted the students to feel comfortable enough to take educational and emotional risks. I accomplished these goals through many community-building activities that helped to launch the year in a fun and creative way. Sometimes other teachers or a young inexperienced principal would question my routine in those first weeks of the year."

Sometimes colleagues were skeptical of her emphasis on community building. "Are you spending any time at all on academics?" one said to her. Another said, "I'm surprised you let them spend so much time having fun. Aren't you worried they're gonna fall behind?" But after all those years, she knew the time spent helping them feel like a group would pay off, ten times over, down the road. So she didn't let those comments bother her.

Margo sometimes overheard her colleagues fret about students who were whiny, lazy, or entitled. They rarely blamed the kids themselves. Instead, they tended to assume such obnoxious behavior could be traced back to parents who hovered over them or treated them like delicate flowers who needed constant tender loving care. One time a friend of Margo's who taught sixth grade said about an annoying student in his class who came across as arrogant and boastful, "His mom must have told him his shit was gold." But sometimes her colleagues said the exact opposite, shaking their heads and mentioning kids whose parents didn't seem to care at all. "They don't come to parent conferences. They probably never eat dinner with her. I bet they haven't attended the science fair in years. That poor kid; I don't know why parents like that even have kids." And then there were the parents who, according to teachers, were just too involved, too whipped up. "I can tell his father helps him with every single assignment. I'll bet that little boy never gets a moment's peace. Why does he have to get 100 percent on everything? They should let that kid just goof off once in a while."

Margo always felt uneasy with these judgments. She had two kids of her own. She knew how hard it was to steer one's children through school. There were so many different ways to misstep, and it was hard to know which mistakes mattered and which didn't. It was OK to forget to send in lunch money, but not OK to miss field day. You shouldn't overpraise your children. But they needed to feel good about themselves. It was important to insist your child got the special help in reading she needed, but not OK to badger the teacher. And one man's badgering was another's advocating. Parenting was filled with small land mines. But she also knew that her colleagues weren't totally wrong. Parents do have a big impact on their children, and not all of it is beneficial. Some of that impact comes via genetics, and there's nothing any of us can do about it. But genes are not the only way parents influence their children's future.

Four Types of Parenting

Psychologist Diana Baumrind (1967) showed that parents vary on two important dimensions: how nurturing or warm they are with their children and the standards they hold their children to. Baumrind found that most parents fell into one of four quadrants:

	Accepting/Responsive	Rejecting/Unresponsive
Demanding	Authoritative/reciprocal	Authoritarian/unresponsive
Undemanding	Indulgent	Neglecting

FIGURE 5-1 *Parenting grid derived from Baumrind*

Parents who were warm, accepting their children for who they were and responding to their children's specific needs and interests, were labeled authoritative. Such parents made it clear what was OK or not OK when it came to the way their child treated others (parents, friends, relatives, and siblings), household responsibilities, and schoolwork. But authoritative parents also showed admiration for their children's particular strengths and achievements, as well as making it clear they understood when their children struggled. Observers saw a give-and-take between these parents and their children (Baumrind 1967).

But some parents who were warm and supportive didn't hold their children to high standards, instead allowing their children to do whatever they wanted. Quick to praise accomplishments and acknowledge their children's distinctive personalities, such parents seemed oblivious to transgressions, overlooking the times their children didn't follow through, didn't try hard, or screwed up. Dr. Baumrind labeled such parents indulgent.

Some parents, on the other hand, rarely showed their children affection, complimented them, or seemed attentive to their feelings and thoughts. Meanwhile, they demanded a lot from their kids. They made it clear they expected high grades, politeness, obedience, and help from their children at home. Quick to punish or criticize, they held back when it came to compliments or validation. Baumrind labeled these parents authoritarian.

Finally, the research showed that another cluster of parents weren't affectionate, but they weren't demanding either. They seemed psychologically removed from their children across the board—preoccupied, uninterested, and often detached. She called these parents neglectful.

Having sorted parents into these quadrants, Baumrind and her colleagues also collected data on the children's behavior in school. The research showed that the children of authoritarian and neglectful parents had all kinds of social and academic problems during elementary and high school. They had trouble with authority, getting along with other children, and making progress in learning. The children most likely to flourish at school were those whose parents fell into the upper left-hand quadrant. Parents like this were affectionate; they hugged, they complimented, and they enjoyed their children. But they also made it clear that they had high standards. They readily celebrated their children's accomplishments and made them feel acknowledged, heard, and appreciated. But they also paid attention to whether their children were doing what was expected—trying hard, sticking with difficult tasks, being kind to others, and doing what they were asked at home. When kids screwed up, parents like this were kind but handed out firm consequences.

It is no wonder teachers periodically grumble about parents. After all, teachers are the ones who are professionally accountable for working with all kinds of rebellious, disorganized, grouchy, sluggish, and unmotivated students. It is their job to ensure that all those children get along with others, follow rules, and learn a long list of skills and information. But over the years Margo had come to realize that even if she was right in guessing what kind of home life a child had (and often she found that her guess was not quite right, that things were more complicated than her instincts told her), what good did it do her? She still had to work with the child, and she couldn't change most children's relationships with their parents, even when she thought she knew what needed changing.

At some point Margo began to wonder what it would be like if she and her colleagues sorted themselves, as teachers, on Baumrind's grid. God knows, she often felt the weight of that old phrase *in loco parentis*—in the place of a parent. She did feel responsible for the kids, and for the year they spent in her class, they were hers. She thought about her students at night. She fretted when one of them began to slide backward. She burst with pride when one of them had a breakthrough.

But that was not all. She also minded terribly when things went wrong. Just as parents can feel ashamed, angry, and frustrated when their child gets in trouble, fails at something, or falls apart, teachers feel badly when their students don't progress. They too take it personally. They too devote a great deal of time and energy to their students, and like parents, they too feel responsible for children's successes and failures. Given the parallels, perhaps teachers could be sorted according to how responsive and warm they were and how clearly they were holding each student to high standards. Perhaps it mattered as much for teachers to be authoritative (rather than authoritarian, permissive, or neglectful) as it did for parents. Margo thought, with relief, that for the most part, she was warm and demanding. But maybe not for every kid. She kept wondering how she was doing with PJ. Just like a spider, Margo was busy weaving a relationship with each of her students. And just as parents have complicated feelings about their kids, so did she.

"As I recall, all of my other students were very engaged and excited about the new classroom, teacher, and fellow students—that is, all but PJ. Throughout those first few weeks, he remained distant and disengaged, and his behavior bordered on disrespect without totally crossing the line. It was a difficult start to the year. PJ caused me much concern and disappointment. I would go home each night and think about the day. What had I done, said, or not done or not said to try to break down the barrier between me and PJ, and the rest of the students and PJ?"

Margo was hard on herself, trying to figure out what she had done wrong, what had kept her from getting through to PJ. But, concerned as she felt, she was on the wrong track. Though deeply gifted, and armed with years of wise experience, she was too close to the situation to see what was really going on. By October, PJ had become that year's problem student. He was keeping her up at night, as she tried to figure out why he seemed so angry yet detached, so reluctant to become part of the group, and so resistant to her. As she tossed and turned, pondering PJ's difficulties, the key to the solution dangled unseen right in front of her. *She was thinking about him.* And that psychological connection to him, however vexed, lay at the heart of the matter.

> *Just as parents can feel ashamed, angry, and frustrated when their child gets in trouble, fails at something, or falls apart, teachers feel badly when their students don't progress. They too take it personally. They too devote a great deal of time and energy to their students, and like parents, they too feel responsible for children's successes and failures.*

Connect, Connect, Connect

Emotional connections with other people begin, for most of us, when we travel through the birth canal. Under ordinary circumstances, as a woman gives birth to a baby, her body produces oxytocin, a hormone that induces intense feelings of attachment (quite a few female mammals produce oxytocin when they mate, and some research suggests that human females produce it when they experience orgasm; some researchers think this helps account for the kind of pair bonding that characterizes humans, voles, and a few other mammals who mate for life). This biological event means that, by and large, newborns spend their first weeks and months being held and fed by someone who is awash in a bath of attachment chemicals. But the mother is not the only one who feels attached. Babies do their part in creating this powerful bond.

Ethologist Konrad Lorenz long ago identified the features of the newborn that attract care from adults: large head, round face, and big eyes all make a baby seem cute, irresistible even. Marc Bornstein (2002) describes that cluster of features as "anatomical competence." Babies who arrive blessed with a healthy dose of those characteristics are more able to get the care they need. When their endless crying grates on an overworked parent, or makes the parent want to flee, that anatomical competence is often what brings the parent back to the vulnerable little baby's side. Babies who, for one reason or another, lack those characteristics (for instance, babies born with fetal alcoholic effects whose heads are narrow and whose eyes take up less room in their face) struggle to get what they need from the grown-ups around them. But their features are just one component. Research has also shown that within hours of birth, babies turn more quickly toward the sound of their mother's voice than they do toward other human voices. In other words, babies arrive wired to prefer the person to whom they are attached. And that's only the first strand in the powerful bond that connects a baby to her caregiver.

The connection that human babies and their caregivers establish has enormous consequences, which last long beyond the first few months. The psychological impact of the link between mother and child was first described by British physician John Bowlby during World War II. Visiting orphanages in London, where babies whose parents were away in the war were being cared for, Bowlby saw that many were doing poorly on almost all measures of infant health and progress. They weren't gaining weight, they were listless, they weren't meeting important intellectual milestones, and they seemed emotionally withdrawn. These care facilities were nothing like some of horrible places documented in recent times, where babies are neglected, hungry, and sometimes abused. The babies in the British orphanages were well fed, clean, and cared for by kind, skilled nurses. But there were many nurses, and needless to say they came and went. In other words, though all of the infants' basic biological needs were being met, they didn't spend sustained time with one constant caregiver. His observations of those babies led to Bowlby's monumental work on the role of attachment and loss in children's development (1972). He argued that in order to grow and thrive psychologically as well as physically, babies require a relationship with one particular caregiver, someone with whom he or she can form a deep emotional bond. Once this idea took hold in the minds of psychologists, it quickly became apparent that attachment was a complex phenomenon. Among other things, it seemed clear that not all attachments were the same.

Mary Ainsworth (Ainsworth et al. 2015), a student of Bowlby's, thought that there might be individual differences not just in the strength of the attachments, but in the kinds of attachments children and adults formed. Just as importantly, Ainsworth thought that the different kinds of attachment could be measured. To test her speculation, she set up one of the most ingenious and famous experiments in child development. She reasoned that simply watching mothers and babies spend time together might not reveal important differences between them. How would one know, just from observing them together for a few moments, what was really going on? To glean something about the quality of attachment, she thought, she'd need to disrupt it in some way. To this end, she invited mothers and their babies, one pair at a time, into a room with some toys (in some versions of the experiments, a stranger was also present). Ainsworth and her colleagues watched each pair through a one-way mirror. Just as she predicted, most behaved in fairly similar ways for the first few moments as the baby explored the toys and the mother sat nearby watching. But then, after a few minutes, the mother, as instructed, left the room. The researchers then watched to see how each baby would react to being left alone (or with a stranger). Here, they began to notice some marked differences in how the children handled the separation. Finally, after a few moments, the mothers reentered the room. The researchers observed this too through the one-way mirror. What the researchers saw when the babies were left alone, and then when they were reunited with their moms, told a vivid story about individual differences in attachment.

Many of the babies seemed, upon entering the room, to be very interested in the toys. The ones who could walk marched over, plopped themselves down, and began exploring. The others crawled and inched. Many of them looked at their mother periodically, or listened if the mother commented in some way on what they were doing. And when she left the room, many looked alarmed, cried in protest, and then sobbed in fear and sadness when she closed the door. When she came back in just moments later, those babies would light up with a relieved and ebullient smile, hurry over to her, and bury themselves into her chest. After a few moments of touching, smiling, or nursing, having reassured themselves of her presence, they'd scramble out of her lap and return to their investigation of the toys. Ainsworth labeled these children *securely attached.*

But not all the babies followed this pattern. Some, who also seemed interested in the toys at first, and then terribly distressed when their mother left the room, reacted differently. They might rush over to their mom, but instead of snuggling happily, they'd seem agitated or even angry. Some kept crying, or hit or pinched their mother, and were unable to really rejoice in her return. Many of these children did finally return to the toys but found it difficult to plunge back into playing. Instead they kept looking up at their mother, distracted by the worry that they would be left alone again. These babies were labeled "anxious" or "insecure."

Finally there were a small number of children who seemed to barely notice when their mother left the room and equally unexcited by her return. They didn't seem all that interested in their mother at any point. Ainsworth described these babies as *detached.* Over the years, since that landmark research was conducted, many researchers have built on the original findings. Scientists have compared children in different cultures and found that while the detached style seemed to spell trouble for children in the United States, in some cultures where child care is a collective enterprise, many of the babies and parents could be characterized as having a detached bond, yet those children didn't seem to suffer negative consequences as they grew older. Perhaps even though attachment begins as a biological and universal process, particular customs and views within a culture play a role in the way it unfolds. Researchers have also tracked children in order to see what, if anything, their classification during toddlerhood might predict about them later on. These studies have shown that the quality of a person's attachment has a very long reach. For instance, children who seem insecurely attached at fifteen months are more likely to be anxious in school and have difficulty developing new friendships. And its reach extends even beyond childhood. A fifteen-month-old who exhibits an anxious attachment to his mother is likely to repeat some of his anxious behaviors even years later, when he is grown and has romantic partners. But it's not only their school friendships and love lives that can be traced back to their early attachment style. Recall that in the original research, the securely attached babies were more able to settle down after their mother's return and explore the toys in the room, while anxious babies had trouble enjoying the interesting new environment. Researchers now believe that secure attachment predicts an interest in the outside world and an appetite for exploration. Every child walks into a classroom carrying with her the powerful imprint of early relationships.

Often young nursery school or kindergarten teachers can feel flustered and frustrated by the four-year-old who sobs each morning when his mom leaves the classroom. They wish the parents had done more to prepare their child for school. The father who, agonized by his son's tears, lingers with uncertainty in the doorway, can be exasperating. When she was young, Margo had fulfilled one of her student teaching practicums in a kindergarten. One little girl clung to her mother each morning as if she were about to get surgery. Her mother was distraught to see her little girl, whom just a few short years before she had nursed night and day, so miserable. It seemed they were feeling the same acute misery. On the eighth day of that new school year, young Margo had left the kindergarten room at lunchtime to use the bathroom. She found the mom still there, huddled on the staircase just outside of the classroom, trying to hear whether her daughter sounded OK. At twenty-two, Margo had had no idea how to handle that mother's anxiety.

It's only natural that a teacher, working with twenty or more children at a time, can feel stymied by the intense interactions they witness between parents and children. Some teachers come up with specific techniques for helping moms leave: a timer, so both child and parent know that after three minutes, the bell will ring and that means it's time to say goodbye, or a small ritual, like reading a short book together or singing a favorite song before separating. Often the key is in making more of a bridge between home and school. A teacher who holds the hand of the forlorn child each morning as her mother waves goodbye doesn't prolong or give in to the problem. She addresses it. That's because underneath what appears to be a difficulty is a healthy sign of development. It's natural to feel pain when you are separated from the person to whom you have been so intimately attached. The kids who don't have a strong attachment during the first years are the ones who may be in real trouble. It's not that every child needs to show distress when he comes to school. But it's perfectly normal if he does. And a child's attachment with a parent is a foundational building block of his or her future. But it's not the end of the story because the relationship children build with a teacher can also have a tremendous impact. For most children, it is the first powerful relationship they have with an adult to whom they are not related. It provides an intellectual and emotional bridge to the world beyond family. Which brings us back to Margo and PJ.

"I called colleagues to discuss my frustration, spoke to the school adjustment counselor, met with his mother, and learned about his interests. With all of that support and information one would think I could have found the key, the right key, to unlock the secret as to how to reach this boy who was obviously so lost inside. Every morning I would enter the classroom thinking that today would be the breakthrough day and every morning he would enter the classroom and stand silently throughout our morning activities, class meetings, and the beginning of our first lesson, until his aide would escort him to the resource room for reading and writing instruction. Then one morning, sometime in late October, PJ spoke up and said quite loudly, for all to hear, 'Ms. Madison, are you aware of the fact that you don't *walk* around the classroom? You *stomp*.' Of course all of the other fourth graders thought this was quite funny and I joined in on the laughter. But considering the fact that I am a relatively slight person with small feet, and rarely if ever wear heavy boots in the classroom, I became very self-conscious of my movements." Like all teacher-student dealings, Margo's interactions with PJ were never particularly private. Whatever he said and did was said and done in front of the other kids. However she reacted also had an audience of twenty-five nine- to ten-year-olds. A classroom is filled with books and equipment and tables. But it's also filled with other developing children. And that is an essential, though sometimes overlooked, component of psychological growth.

Development Is Not Solitary

When Piaget did his groundbreaking observations of children, all of his attention was focused on the ways in which their interactions with objects around them shaped their thoughts. A close read of his work shows that he envisioned intellectual development as a process by which the child came to understand the mathematical and scientific principles that underlie our world. In other words, he saw children as budding scientists. But he overlooked a great deal of what must have been going on during those observations. Because it's obvious to anyone now that children are as deeply engaged with the world of people as they are with the world of objects. And it's not just that they argue, hug, grab, and laugh with others. They also spend a great deal of their time studying the people around them. They are as eager to absorb the rules that govern social interactions as they are the rules that govern the natural world. All the time that they are constructing hypotheses about number, balance, and volume, they are also acquiring equally powerful insights about how people interact. They experiment with the best ways to get what they want, how to influence others, and what is valued and not valued among the grown-ups around them. Nor are they only interested in *using* other people. They also become interested in how and what other people think.

To take one very important example of the way in which young children study others, consider the child's dawning awareness of other people's minds. The very idea that each person has a separate mind filled with distinct beliefs would be far beyond the comprehension of any three-year-old. Yet by the time children are five, they seem to know that other people may think differently than they do. They also seem to understand that what another person knows, believes, or intends to do is based on the information she has, which may or may not be the same as their own. Take, for instance, the classic version of this concept in *Little Red Riding Hood*. In the story, Little Red Riding Hood knocks on her grandmother's door and thinks the creature who opens it is her grandmother (with strangely big eyes and teeth). When four-year-olds read this story, they think that Little Red Riding Hood knows it is the wolf because they know it's the wolf. They don't yet have the capacity to see that Little Red Riding Hood doesn't have access to the same information they, the readers, do. But by five most children will quickly acknowledge that two people can have different thoughts or intentions because they've had access to different sets of information. Psychologists refer to this as "theory of mind." Theory of mind is what makes it possible to guess what another person will do, what he thinks, and what his beliefs are. It allows people to appreciate more than one perspective, not just of an object, but also of an argument. It is central to many kinds of complex thinking (Harris 2012).

This shift to a theory of mind is not just a cognitive accomplishment; it also signals the child's increasing interest in understanding the minds and behaviors of those around her. Once children have a theory of mind, most become eager to understand the thoughts of others. Studying the minds of others provides them with essential information about the way the world works. Psychologists now believe that children are not only budding scientists, as Piaget led us to believe, but also budding anthropologists. To complicate this strand of intellectual growth even more, it turns out that the two worlds of knowledge, social and natural, are not always as separate from one another as one might think.

Once children have a theory of mind, most become eager to understand the thoughts of others. Studying the minds of others provides them with essential information about the way the world works.

Seeing the World Together

Soon after they are born, children begin experiencing the physical world around them through the eyes and ears of those they love and trust. When something surprising, new, or complex happens, like a stranger entering the room or something crashing to the floor, babies will often watch the object or event for a second, turn and study their mother's reaction to that same object or event, and then look back at the object themselves. Colwyn Trevarthen argued that by viewing the world along with their mothers or fathers, young children's thoughts and knowledge about the world are, from the beginning, filtered through the minds of other people. He called this shared contemplation of the world intersubjectivity (Trevarthen and Aitken 2001). Babies and their parents don't simply view the same object or event; they *share* their thoughts about the object.

In the last twenty years a great deal of research has expanded on this idea that children don't simply develop as separate individuals, with private knowledge, acquired via solo activity. Instead, children's thoughts emerge with and in the company of other people—parents, babysitters, teachers, and grandparents. But it's not only adults who shape a child's mental growth. Peers are also key to intellectual development.

Michael Tomasello and his colleagues' experiments show that even at age four children learn from one another, spontaneously sharing knowledge and skills. For instance, in one ingenious set of studies, they taught a four-year-old a technique for retrieving a small toy from a clear plastic box (a bit like the ones that stand outside big stores or at carnivals), a method that no children come up with on their own (Flynn and Whiten 2010, Tomasello 2014). Then they placed the box in the child's classroom. Within three days, virtually all of the children had learned the technique. Typically the target child would teach one or two others how to retrieve the prize. Then those children would teach one or two others. Tomasello's studies have shown that knowledge isn't just transmitted vertically (from adult to child) but also horizontally (from one child to another). The research of Tomasello and others provides data to support the ideas first put forth by Lev Vygotsky in the early 1900s: cognitive development is a cultural process.

There was a lot going on between Margo and PJ. But they weren't alone in the classroom. There were twenty-five other students with them. And those twenty-five other ten-year-olds were participating fully, if often from the sidelines, as PJ and Margo's relationship unfolded. Information, attitudes, and personal development aren't always or only between the teacher and the student. As the research of Tomasello and Trevarthen shows, children are often developing ideas with other children.

Margo continued talking to the teachers at the workshop. "Now as I tell you this, it sounds very silly to me. But for some reason this caused me to become very self-aware of how I walked, and this self-awareness stayed with me for the remainder of the year. I would find myself tiptoeing around the classroom whenever he was present, like a ballerina in glass slippers, fearing they would shatter if I stepped down too hard." Margo saw that the other children stopped what they were doing whenever she and PJ had one of their exchanges. They noticed that PJ periodically went after Margo. That he seemed to want to challenge her. They found it entertaining. But it put them on edge. How would she handle his comments, which were right on the edge of rude? She rarely took the bait from a ten-year-old. But as she admitted to the group of teachers, his comment about her stomping had stung. She felt sure that a few of his classmates noticed her change in gait.

We tend to think about how adults shape and affect their students. And they do. But it is rarely a one-way dynamic. As Margo's story reveals, children have a powerful effect on their teachers as well. And this too is a natural part of development. Recall that when babies are born, their mothers get a strong dose of oxytocin, the hormone involved in feelings of love and attachment. It's not just that babies feel attached to their mothers. Mothers feel attached to their babies. In fact, the work of Dan Stern (1977) shows that at its best, mothers and babies are so involved with one another that they engage in what he called a dance. Using split-screen films, Stern and his colleagues showed that mothers and babies are highly attuned to one another—when the baby's voice rises, the mother might lift her eyebrows and open her mouth, matching in pace, tone, or intensity the baby's voice. When the mother lifts her hands up, the baby may respond in kind using her legs. Stern and others have argued that the nearly exquisite coordination and responsiveness of mother and baby are critical to healthy cognitive social and emotional development. When babies and their mothers are not well attuned (which can happen for any number of reasons, like depression, substance abuse, or just a powerful mismatch in temperament), there are long-term psychological consequences. And, like attachment, attunement between teachers and their students is as important as between parents and their children. Jennie and George were a perfect example of that.

Love in the Classroom

Jennie Miro was tall and willowy. She had fine straight hair that fell to her chin, framing her angular face in a way that was somehow both plain and chic. She looked young and hip, and she was. And she had a low-key, offhand way of talking to her second graders that worried parents. They thought it meant the kids would run wild in her classroom, that she was too young to be effective. In fact, she had command over every group she worked with. Though young, she had always felt easily in charge. Like Margo, she knew that connecting with her students was essential. And it came easily to her.

George was not the only bubbly kid she had in her second-grade classroom. And he wasn't the only one who loved school or was good at it. Each year, in her school just outside of Chicago, she worked with bright, energetic kids who wanted to learn (though she had plenty who weren't so bright, or didn't want to learn, as well). But George was by far the most intellectually intense child she had encountered in her first four years of teaching. It wasn't that he was good at reading, math, or science experiments. It wasn't that he jumped into each project and group activity with verve. (Though he did all of those things.) She quickly saw that he yearned for something beyond the fun and challenging activities she offered her second graders each day; he craved intellectual exchange, and he sought it from her. He'd ask her questions like, "Do you think if there were people on Saturn they would age the same way people on Earth do?" And here is where Jennie's attunement to George made all the difference. She didn't know about Saturn. Luckily that didn't bother her at all. In fact, it delighted her. She couldn't resist George's curiosity, and she wanted to be part of his intellectual journey. She tried to find information in the books they had in the classroom (this was long before the world of Google). She asked him if he could think of anyone who could help them answer the question. He thought maybe his brother Paul, who was nine years older than he, could help. Paul, age seventeen, sent in the following note. "Dear Miro: According to Einstein's theory of relativity, the less strong the gravitational force, the slower you age. The example Stephen Hawking gives, in *A Brief History of Time*, is of two twins, of the same exact age, down to the second, separated at birth, one living on a high mountain, the other on a low plain; by the time one hundred years had passed the one living on the high mountain would be younger, technically. This theory was tested with an atomic clock in a plane. George was telling me about your discussion about Saturn and age. So though you would be younger in Saturn years, compared to someone on Earth, you would actually have been older because the gravitational force is stronger on Saturn than here on Earth. I wish I was in your class. Sincerely yours, Paul (George's older brother)."

Anyone reading this note might notice how nice it was that an older brother was interested enough to send in that note. Any reader might be impressed that a second grader cared enough to come home and ask his brother the question. But a careful reader would also notice that Paul addressed the note simply to Miro. Not Miss or Ms. Miro. Not even Jennie. It turned out that though all the other eighty-plus students Jennie had taught so far had called her Ms. Miro, George skipped the *Ms.* and called her just Miro.

Asked about it years later, Jennie said she had no idea why George had called her Miro. As she recalled, he had started addressing her that way within the first week of class. She thought it was funny. Her impulse was to take her students' lead whenever she could, so she had simply responded to him as if nothing were out of the ordinary. It was just one more link in the special connection they formed. She had made it a habit to find small points of connection with each of her students. Something she and a child both loved or both hated. Splitting a cookie on Fridays with a student who brought in her favorite raisin cookies. A mutual love of the White Sox baseball team. She knew that humor and small shared rituals would go far in helping her reach each child.

For nearly twenty years she kept the note from George's brother Paul in a large box of important teaching materials. It wasn't a note of appreciation or admiration to her. It wasn't a memento of her student's success and thus wasn't an obvious emblem of her successful teaching. Instead, keeping it was her way of saving the connection to George.

Many years later, George's mother came across a folder of materials from George's school days. Buried in among her four children's drawings, book reports, and grades was a photograph someone had taken of Miro and George. In the photograph the two of them are standing alone in the classroom. Jennie is dressed in her usual corduroys and loose cardigan. Seven-year-old George is wearing the very small blue jeans and orange sweatshirt he wore to school nearly every day throughout second grade. But in the photograph, they are also both wearing full-on snorkeling gear: flippers, masks, and snorkels. They are standing close together, six-foot slender woman, three-foot compact boy, gazing steadily at the camera. The photo is whimsical and alluring. And it is also mysterious. Why was George wearing snorkeling gear in the middle of winter in his Midwest, landlocked neighborhood? Why was his second-grade teacher also wearing flippers, a mask, and a snorkel? What stands out in the photo, and in the memories of all involved (George, Paul, their mother, and Jennie herself), is that in order for Jennie to be the best teacher she could to this bright, intense little boy, she had to have a specific, unique bond with him. She had to be as attached to him as he was to her.

Years later, when Jennie came across the note George's brother Paul had sent in, she thought back to a conversation that she had had with her supervisor, during her first year of teaching. She had come to her supervisor worried about one little boy, Sasha. He'd had trouble reading and seemed remote and tense—hard to reach. And if she was honest with herself, she'd found him annoying. Eager to overcome her weaknesses, she had said to her supervisor, "I think I am doing a bad job with Sasha; I can't find anything to love about him."

Her supervisor, an experienced teacher with thirty-one years in the classroom, had tilted her head skeptically with an expression on her face as if Jennie had started speaking in Sanskrit. "What? You don't need to find something to love about him. You just need to teach him." But now, years later, Jennie realized that in order to teach a child you *did* have to find something to love about him or her. If you weren't attached, how could the child be? And if there was no attachment, a large raft of essential things wouldn't and couldn't happen in the classroom.

One year when Margo was assigned to a second-grade classroom, she taught a pistol of a student named Owen. Owen was haywire at least a third of the time. He often just gyrated out of control in group discussions, fell off his chair in agitation during any kind of solitary focused work, picked fights, and often had a runny nose and a tear in his clothes. He was a mess, inside and out. But he was also smart, warm, and engaging. Margo was exasperated by him. She found that her usual gentle and subtle ways of managing kids didn't work with Owen. In fact, as the year went on, he seemed to be getting wilder. Finally another teacher suggested that every time he misbehaved, she should put a check up in the right-hand corner of her blackboard. When he got three checks, he'd lose a few minutes of his recess. Margo resisted this approach. It seemed punitive and superficial somehow. But she was at her wits' end, so finally she thought she'd give it a try. She explained to Owen what the plan was. He watched her solemnly as she wrote OWEN in thick capital letters in the upper right-hand corner of the blackboard right behind her desk. Over the next few days, each time he'd push, shout, or throw his paper across the room, she'd look at him, then walk over to the board, and carefully make a check near his name. Each time it happened, he watched her, and if she didn't know better, she'd say he had a little smile on his face. Not a smirk, more like a look of contentment. His outbursts dwindled just a bit, not a lot. She didn't know why, but the check marks just became a quiet little communication between them, something they both leaned on as an aid in their coexistence. That year, Margo was pregnant with her first child. She announced to her students in March that after the April vacation they would have a new teacher for the last six weeks of the year. One day in early April, when her stomach was sticking far out, and she was just counting the days until her maternity leave, she asked her students to line up to go out for recess. Owen, standing in the front of the line, as always, suddenly looked up at her and said in a loud, impulsive voice, "If the baby dies, will you come back after vacation?" She was appalled and upset by the question. But later that night, she realized that Owen didn't say it to be mean or express hostility. Quite the opposite. He was just worried about his impending separation from her. It was then that she realized why he seemed to like watching her make the check marks on the board. It was a sign to him that she was thinking about him. Even though it wasn't a technique she'd like to use again, it taught her something about Owen.

Even Subtle Connections Have an Impact

Margo knew that her relationship with each student was every bit as important as the curriculum she developed or the routines she used to help her children become more skilled at school. That's why PJ, as withdrawn and hostile as he often seemed, haunted her so. Margo stood in front of the teachers, winding up her presentation.

"I wish this story had a happy ending, but regardless of all my efforts, I was unable to connect with PJ. I guess in every fish story, there is always the one that gets away, but as a teacher who loves her students so much, I didn't take the failure well. He left in June with me still thinking about what I could have done differently, and that is not to say that he didn't excel, and his mother wasn't happy with his experience in my classroom, but I knew it could have been better if I had just been able to reach him.

"Two years ago I was at a local musical event and spotted PJ in the crowd, proudly wearing an usher's uniform. Our eyes met and he nodded his head in recognition and gave me a slight smile, and I found myself tiptoeing past him on the way to my seat."

Margo had chosen to share this story because in her mind, it was important to show younger, newer teachers that there will always be a student you cannot reach. She wanted to help them accept the fact that they wouldn't succeed with every student. That somehow he had gotten under her skin, but she hadn't gotten under his. But the truth was different than that. If noticing what a child thinks and mattering enough to him that he notices things about you reflects attachment, Margo had certainly reached PJ. And he had reached her. She thought about him, and he thought about her. They were connected. Was it an easy attachment? No. Did it leave either of them feeling calm and confident? Probably not. But they had influenced one another. Each relationship a child forms adds a layer to his or her emerging self. Perhaps Margo hadn't transformed PJ, or gotten him to fall in love with reading or math. But she had contributed to his growth. And he to hers. After the presentation, one of the young teachers, named Ivan, came up to her. It seemed he lived next door to PJ's older sister, who was married with children. "I know PJ!" he told her. "He's seventeen now, and he's a car mechanic. He's still sort of like the way you described him. Kind of stiff. But it's funny. I know you told us that story so that we could understand that we can't succeed with every kid we teach. But last time PJ came by to see his sister, we were all sitting around talking about our old school days. He was saying he never liked school too much. Then he said that there was only one teacher he still thought about—his fourth-grade teacher. It was you! He said you were the one who really 'got' him. And that's something, coming from PJ."

CHAPTER SIX

Charlie and Marley

◆

```
Emergence of the Self * Self-Control *
Self-Expression
```

MS. KANE COULDN'T believe it when she looked down at her class list, then up at the seven-year-old faces staring back at her on that first day of school in September. But it was true. She had a Charlie and a Marley in the group. They had comically rhyming names. As if it weren't enough to have those two names in the same group, they also happened to gravitate toward one another. Over the next few days, she couldn't help but watch the two. What an unlikely duo.

Charlie: Upbeat and Out of Control

Charlie had light hazel eyes and shiny black hair that sprang up from his scalp and tilted in several different directions. He was a lithe little boy—his body animated and his face expressive. He walked into the classroom each morning on the balls of his feet, bubbling with energy and a look of eager expectation on his face. He often came in talking about one of his current enthusiasms—capoeira, magic tricks, and sharks. Once inside the room, he'd glance around quickly to see what others were doing, searching for the group or game that beckoned to him. But often, within minutes of joining an activity, Charlie's eyes would begin roaming, less absorbed by what was in front of him, scanning the room for what he might be missing out on. At 8:30 Ms. Kane rang her small chime, letting the kids know it was time for reading. By the end of the first week, many of the children seemed already to have memorized most of the routines of the day. So when they heard the chime they'd go to their cubbies, get their reading books, and head to the table for their group. But Charlie didn't always make it. Somewhere along the way, in the five minutes it took the other children to wrap up their free-play activity and get to the table with the assigned reading book, Charlie got distracted. He'd stop by the fish tank, and dip his fingers in the water, seeing if he might be able to touch one of the fish (though he knew that was forbidden). He'd head over to another kid and begin chatting about a magic trick that had stupefied his mother the night before, or he'd stand by the door, watching the fifth graders walk down the hall, calling out to a friend of his older sister. He genuinely liked other people, and his interest in the social world came across loud and clear. Meanwhile, the others were ready to start their daily reading.

Ms. Kane, who was in her late thirties, had a warm, approachable face, an appealingly husky voice, and a calm manner. She would patiently remind Charlie where he should be. Perhaps, she thought, he'd just take a little more time than the other children to get used to the new routines of first grade. She always gave her students the benefit of the doubt. Charlie was such a friendly kid, and he seemed perfectly happy to be put back on track. Each time Ms. Kane reminded him, he'd cheerily grab his reader and join his group. Sometimes Ms. Kane had the children in a group read aloud to one another while she or her assistant listened in. Some days she had them read quietly to themselves and answer a short worksheet of simple questions about what they were reading. Other times she had the children identify particular letters, sounds, or parts of the sentences. No matter what they did during reading time, Charlie rarely stayed with the task for long. Within a minute or so one leg would begin to swing wildly under the table, his eyes would slide away from the text, and instead of reading, he'd doodle on the side of the page with his pencil. By the third week, Ms. Kane was a little less understanding. Charlie's fidgeting and distraction were disruptive to the other kids and to her routines. But perhaps more worrisome, his squirming and chitchat were keeping him from making much progress. If she didn't begin reining him in, he'd lose ground academically.

Marley: Too Calm?

Meanwhile, Marley was another ball of wax altogether. His skin was so pale it was almost translucent, and his fine brown hair lay flat on his head. He had a small sprinkle of freckles across his nose. He too was slender, but not buoyant like Charlie. He seemed more measured, more self-contained. When he walked, his arms hung down by his sides, like a grown-up. On that first day, while Charlie was bobbing up and down between the book stacks, his cubby, and the fish tank, Marley was watching, taking stock of Ms. Kane and the group dynamic. He studied the others with a slightly unreadable look on his face. He wasn't nervous and Ms. Kane saw no signs that he felt left out. He was just an observer. When he had first arrived he had carefully perused the cubbies, found the one with his name on it, walked right over to it, neatly put away his lunch box and pencils, and hung his sweatshirt on the hook. He seemed already, at seven, to have the school routine down pat.

On that first day, when Marley quickly and quietly took his seat, Charlie was still scanning the room, stretching his neck, checking out all the many options. But once his eyes rested on Marley, it was as if he had heard a silent signal: "This is your mate." He walked right over and took the seat next to Marley and began chatting with him. A very small smile lifted the edges of Marley's mouth. He nodded at whatever Charlie was saying to him with such animation. Ms. Kane was pulling various books from a bookshelf and watching the children get settled. She saw that Charlie and Marley meshed instantly, talking as if they were picking up on a stream of conversation that had been going on for years.

But once Ms. Kane rang her chime and started explaining what would happen on that first day, the two boys seemed, ever so slightly, to lean away from one another. While Charlie cased the joint and tapped his foot, Marley let his hands fall to his sides, where they lay still, and studied the teacher's face as she spoke. Ms. Kane explained that they would always begin the day with reading. She then walked around writing down on her clipboard what each child had chosen as his or her first reading book. The whole time she was speaking, Marley kept his eyes on her face. When she came over to him, he promptly reached out to take his book quietly, perusing the cover, then opening to the first page to see how his story began. Later, when Ms. Kane thought about Marley, she realized she had barely noticed his seamless mastery of those first routines. Though Ms. Kane's antenna had begun to quiver about Charlie's inattention, the only thing that caught her attention in those first weeks, about Marley, was his friendship with Charlie. They were such a little team. Charlie would find Marley each morning as soon as he got to school. The nearly black curls would bend toward the straight dirty blond hair, and they'd exchange tidbits from home—who had played soccer, whether each had brought pizza money, and what had happened on the school bus. Ms. Kane realized that they always stood next to one another when it was time to line up and were always together on the playground. She could see that Marley enjoyed Charlie. When Charlie was at his most animated, Marley would look up every once in a while from his work to see what Charlie was up to. He'd watch him for a moment, the corners of his lips turned up with pleasure. And Charlie? Even though he was the livelier and louder of the two, he sought Marley out. Ms. Kane wondered whether Charlie liked the audience or if it was something deeper. Maybe Charlie found Marley's competence to be comforting. But she was concerned too. Would Charlie's fidgets and disruptions corrupt Marley? Marley seemed like such a good student.

As she did every year, on the Friday of the fourth week of school, Ms. Kane straightened her desk, gathered up her class list and folder, and went to the nearby Roasting House to enjoy a cup of coffee and think over what she had learned about each student. Looking down at her notes, she realized that in the eighteen days of school so far, she had made notes on Charlie's misbehavior 112 times—usually five or six times a day. Sometimes it was for little things—balancing his pencil on the end of his finger when she was giving the group instructions. Sometimes it was for larger things—jumping up during a quiz and running to the window to see what was making a loud noise. One time when he was frustrated because of the way his collage had turned out, he got so upset he tore it up into little pieces which he flung everywhere like confetti. For that she asked him to sit next to her desk in the "cool-down chair" for five minutes. Charlie's fidgets and outbursts didn't seem to be getting better. Contrary to her hopes, Charlie wasn't settling into the routine. And, she realized, he was losing ground academically. While many of the other kids were already on their second chapter book, Charlie was still toiling through the first chapter of the first book he had chosen from the shelf of stories written especially for kids just making the transition to chapter books. It shouldn't have been too challenging. Most of the children had finished the math review pages she'd given to help them get back on track after the long mathless summer, and were already working on the ones and tens places and the reversibility of digits in addition and multiplication. But not Charlie. He should have been flying through the simple addition and subtraction problems that were a repeat of last year. Instead he labored through $5 + 2$ and $6 - 3$ as if each problem were a mountain to climb.

A small cloud collected in her mind. Charlie was going to be a challenge.

Every teacher has at least one Charlie in the classroom, each year. The kid who, at his (or her) best, seems lively, bright, and appealing, but just as often drums his fingers, wiggles in his seat, stares out the window, or talks to others during work time. Sometimes a kid like that has even more irritating and troubling problems—calling out again and again while the teacher is talking, dissolving or exploding in anger and frustration when things are difficult, and losing control when others hurt his feelings. Often kids like this become less likeable, over time, to their teachers and their classmates.

What Does It Really Mean to Have Self-Control?

Though teachers have been dealing with such children ever since there have been schools, in recent years researchers have pinpointed underlying skills that explain the difference between kids like Charlie and kids like Marley (see, for instance, Raver et al. 2011). They've collected those skills under the umbrella term *executive function*. By now this concept is fairly familiar to most educators and often invoked to explain itchy, scatterbrained students. Kids who were once described by teachers, somewhat casually, as being ADD or ADHD now are described as having low EF. But the term is not really meant to be a casual label. Instead, it refers to a specific group of psychological processes. We know much more than we did ten years ago about each of these processes. Charlie was the walking, talking embodiment of what it means for a child to have low executive functioning.

Like many kids who struggle with executive functioning, Charlie often seemed to be all over the place—his tapping leg, darting eyes, frequent outbursts, and bounciness that edged into trouble seemed to be all of a piece. But researchers now think that these behaviors, and the problems they reflect, fall into two distinct psychological clusters, one that depends on the mind, the other more on the gut.

The Mind Cluster

The mind cluster involves focusing, tuning out distractions, and remembering important information or instructions. It also involves integrating that information, making good choices about what to pay attention to, concentrating, and ordering one's thoughts. Imagine, for example, a child who is asked to answer questions on a worksheet about a book while a few other kids are working on their diorama and two kids are in a small meeting with the teacher. That child has to tune out the other activities in the class, concentrate long enough to read the questions on the worksheet, and remember the information learned during previous lessons. She also has to remember that she's done worksheets like this before, and that there is one way to approach the task that makes it easier: read the instructions first, do them in order, fill in her name at the top, and go over it before handing it in. For a child who struggles with any one of these components, a seemingly simple assignment can become overwhelming. It isn't necessarily the content that is too difficult; she may be very bright and able to understand complex information and ideas. She may just not have the psychological tools for harnessing her good thoughts.

In recent years, researchers have gone beyond disentangling these processes from one another. They've also figured out how to measure a child's ability in each individual strand of the cluster. For instance, children vary in how good they are at paying close attention to instructions while simultaneously tuning out alluring sounds or sights that might get in the way of taking in the instructions. To find out just how good a child is at this, researchers use something they call the peg-tapping task. They instruct children to lightly tap a wooden dowel against the tabletop twice whenever the experimenter taps once, and once when the experimenter taps twice (Ursache, Blair, and Raver 2012). The task may sound simple, but it requires children to remember the rule and to suppress the very natural urge to mimic the grown-up. It bears some resemblance to Simon Says. It's not hard to see that the peg-tapping game is a good stand-in for a common requirement of school: ignoring input that may be calling out to you in order to focus on instructions that are less compelling and often difficult. It's like doing what the teacher has asked you to do and ignoring what the kid next to you is saying, or using a new computing method for math instead of the more familiar way you've done it before. Some kids are quite good at the peg-tapping task, others not so much. For each of the more cognitive components of EF, there are ways to measure a child's capacity. Ms. Kane didn't know about the peg-tapping task. But she did know that Charlie, so able to tell a great story to the other kids waiting on line for the bus, seemed to jump into activities without hearing her full instructions. It wasn't that he didn't want to do the work. While she had been talking, he had been staring at two birds fighting over a worm, just outside the window.

The Gut Cluster

To do well in school, kids need more than the ability to filter information, direct their attention, and organize instructions (the strands of the mind cluster). They also need to control their feelings and impulses (the gut cluster). By the time kids are six or so, many have learned that they can't grab things from other children, no matter how irresistible the toy is. Most also quickly learn at school (if they haven't at home) that they have to wait while someone else takes a turn during a game and that you can't just hit or hug someone because you feel like it. Inhibiting impulses is a big part of early development and involves a different kind of psychological process than staying focused on instructions or remembering information. Researchers have devised a different set of tasks to assess these bottom-up skills. For instance, in one such assessment the experimenter asks the child not to peek while she noisily wraps a gift. Here too, the child must control herself and stay focused. But instead of employing intellectual processes, she needs to simply hold back on her urge to look at something really alluring (like a shiny paper or the present inside). Just as the peg-tapping task simulates things like listening to difficult instructions, the no-peeking game mirrors a common challenge in school: not giving in to urges and emotional impulses.

To do well in school, kids need more than the ability to filter information, direct their attention, and organize instructions (the strands of the mind cluster). They also need to control their feelings and impulses (the gut cluster).

Researchers have found that in general, children get more control over their intellectual processes and their urges as they get older (see Zelazo et al. 2003). After all, when Marley was three, he probably obliviously and cheerily marched over and grabbed the shovel from another child because he wanted it to make a cave in the sandbox. But within a few years he had quite easily absorbed the prohibition against grabbing. No one had to teach him that. He wanted to be part of the group, do what was expected, and act more grown-up. And it didn't take deliberate effort on his part; it was pretty easy, as he got older, to hold back, wait his turn, and keep to himself. If you peek inside a kindergarten, and then a fifth-grade classroom, you will instantly see how much more self-control the older children have. Even on the playground, it's apparent, when no one is watching, that by the age of ten or so, most children have undergone a sea change in the way that they manage their own behavior. But on the other hand, if you stay a while, and study how the fifth graders carry themselves around the room, and how they behave during lessons, you'll quickly see that the kids are as different from one another as they are from the kindergartners.

What Marshmallows Can Tell Us

When the kids arrived on the Monday of the second week of school, Ms. Kane had left several baskets of interesting materials—origami paper, colored felt, metallic sheets, yarn, and old scraps of wrapping paper—on a shelf where she kept all the boxes and canvas bags she used to bring in whatever equipment she needed for a specific activity. Some of the kids noticed the bags and asked about it. She said, "Sometime this week we're going to begin doing a fun project with all that stuff, but not until we've finished the chapter we're reading aloud about weather. When we're ready you'll each have a chance to choose some of those materials. But not now; that's why they're still up on the shelf. Please just leave them there. You'll have a chance to look them over later." Marley gazed at the enticing pieces peeking out from the bags, looked over at Ms. Kane, and walked to his seat for reading time. Charlie began to walk toward his seat, too, and then did a quick U-turn back to the shelf with the materials. His hand grazed all the bright colors and came to rest on a particularly luscious piece of purple felt. Ms. Kane called out to him to please take a seat. As he turned to walk to his table, his hand darted back out and grabbed the felt. As she took the felt from him and gave him a gentle nudge toward his seat, she couldn't help but wonder how Marley and Charlie would have done in the famous marshmallow task (Mischel 2014).

By now many know the original experiment that assessed children's ability to delay gratification: the marshmallow task, designed by Walter Mischel in the 1970s. Experimenters asked boys and girls of various ages to sit down at a table on which was placed a tempting marshmallow. The adult then said something like, "Please wait in here for a few minutes. If you don't eat the marshmallow while I'm gone, you can have two to eat when I get back." Then the experimenter left the room, with a camera running to capture how the children would respond.

In video footage, now easily available on YouTube, you can see the intriguing range of reactions children have to such a common dilemma: enjoy a small pleasure right away or wait for bigger pleasure later on. Faced with something even as modest as one little marshmallow, some children seem to have no control at all. In fact, in the videos it appears as if a few children never really register the promise of two marshmallows. The minute the experimenter closes the door, their hands dart out to grab the marshmallow and cram it in their mouths. The looks on their faces are hard to read: pleasure and a shadow of worry that they've transgressed? Maybe. Others have blank looks on their faces, as if all they are thinking about is the marshmallow in their mouths.

But some kids have a longer, more complex struggle. They clearly want to resist the marshmallow. They look at it and tell themselves, out loud, not to eat it. Some look toward the door, as if trying to remember the words of the grown-up or guess how likely she is to come back in right away. A few touch or even stroke the marshmallow. Some tear a little bit off and put it on their tongues, as if they can give in just a little bit now and still get the prize for waiting. Many of those kids are already sunk. Within moments their shaky self-control has evaporated and the marshmallow is gone. That struggle embodies one most of us face all our lives. And certainly children grapple with various versions of the marshmallow task all day long at school.

The Reluctant Crawl Toward Self-Control

Human beings don't start out orderly or self-controlled. Just watch a baby crying when she is uncomfortable—filled with despair and rage, she doesn't care who hears her. Even at two or three, a miserable child will wail in a movie theatre or lie down on the sidewalk. Young children tend to be consumed by their own internal experience. Misery is not the only feeling that consumes them. Just watch babies who have settled down to nurse. They become wrapped in a bubble of pleasurable sensation. A three-year-old enthralled turning the crank on a jack-in-the-box becomes literally ecstatic with excited anticipation.

Human beings don't start out orderly or self-controlled.

Sigmund Freud transformed the way we think about human beings with his insight that we all begin life defined by our needs and governed by our attempts to fulfill those needs. We are not constrained, as infants, by any concerns about other people's feelings, fitting in, or achieving a goal. In a three-year-old, such unconstrained pursuit of one's needs is not a sign of naughtiness or bad upbringing. It's a sign of normalcy. Learning to do what is expected of us, follow rules, and redirect our impulses takes time and experience.

The ferocious drive to fulfill one's needs at all costs soon begins bending to other forces. By the time babies are five months old, many have figured out ways to calm themselves down and make themselves feel better. They use physical techniques— sucking their thumbs, rubbing their hands together, and bouncing. They also begin to distract themselves, looking away from things that distress them and focusing on something pleasurable instead. These are the first signs of the slow march toward managing one's feelings. Over the next seven years or so, children supplement such rudimentary forms of self-regulation with more sophisticated techniques. They learn to push unpleasant thoughts away from consciousness, to launch themselves into activities that they enjoy as a way of withstanding a temptation, and to hold back on impulses of which others disapprove.

Tell a two-year-old he's bothering the other people in the cinema and he'll just cry louder. He couldn't care less, in that moment, how his behavior affects others. His internal feeling far overpowers his concerns for the world around him. Even an orderly boy like Marley probably shrieked loudly with glee in a library or bawled during a wedding ceremony because he was hungry. But over the next four years other forces come into play. By six, children want approval from adults, and they want to fit in with the group. Those drives are growing as mighty as the internal ones. Tell a five-year-old who cares about you that you want him to stop making so much noise or that people just don't cry in the grocery store, and he may well look around him and then simmer down. As children age they generally get better at postponing a small pleasure for the sake of a bigger future reward, whether it's a marshmallow, the approval of a grown-up, or the sense of fitting in. But some, like Charlie, continue to struggle; they find it hard to manage their internal impulses. Even when they are six, eight, or eleven, some children are overcome, again and again, by internal impulses that get them in trouble with the world around them. The key to helping those children can be found in the behaviors of the kids who resisted the marshmallow.

Marshmallow Resisters

Not all very young children succumb to the siren song of small temptations. Some kids as young as five can wait, if they try. Many of the children in the marshmallow studies listened to the adult explain the rules, and after she left the room, sat quietly, with the marshmallow sitting right in front of them, happily accepting their two marshmallows at the end of five or ten minutes. Kids like that listen to instructions, restrain themselves, and then enjoy the rewards of their patience. But just because some kids could resist the treat doesn't mean it was easy for them. They had to *make* themselves wait. Just like the others, these kids *wanted* to eat the sweet that was sitting there calling out to be tasted. It wasn't that they were less tempted. Instead, they used two specific skills to wait it out. They were able to keep in mind the prize. Reminding yourself what you stand to gain is a superb strategy. It provides people with a powerful motivation for controlling their impulses. For the children in these studies, focusing on the reward helped them come up with clever ways to hold off. Their techniques were not all that subtle, either. They hummed and told themselves not to look. They turned their backs so they couldn't see the marshmallow. They played games with their hands to keep from touching or grabbing the treat. They reminded themselves they'd get two very soon. Some chanted a little credo of self-control, "Just wait, just wait, just wait." Kids with good self-control *deliberately* attempt to do what they should and avoid what they should not. And the payoff of such efforts goes way beyond marshmallows.

The Hidden Rewards of Waiting

In 2005, psychologists Angela Duckworth and Martin Seligman showed just how valuable waiting for the marshmallow could be. Instead of marshmallows, Duckworth and Seligman asked middle school students to rate themselves, using a scale from one to seven, on statements like "I always finish my homework before I watch television," "I usually like to relax for a while and do my chores later in the day," and "I usually count to ten when someone makes me angry." Just as kids varied in their ability to hold off with the marshmallows, eleven-year-olds varied in their answers to these questions. And the kids whose performance on Duckworth and Seligman's questionnaires suggested a capacity to wait were also the ones who, in their senior year, had a high GPA and a good score on their college admission tests. Duckworth and Seligman's work upended the long-held belief that the best way to predict a child's future academic success was by finding out how smart he was. Instead, the new work suggested, a test that captured children's level of self-control seemed to offer a better crystal ball. Knowing whether teenagers put work before play, stay focused on a task until it's finished, and tune out temptations and distractions tells you more about their future success than their IQ scores.

You don't have to wait until children are eleven or twelve to find out if they have what it takes to control themselves. You can see it even in a four-year-old. If Ms. Kane had met Charlie when he was four, she might well have detected the signs that he would struggle with focus, impulse control, and the delay of gratification. No doubt he would have been the preschooler who began eating his snack-time cookie before everyone had been served and who shouted out his Secret Santa recipient even when told to keep it secret. But would labeling him sooner have helped? Just because self-discipline predicts academic success, does that mean if you get a child to be more disciplined you can get him to learn more? Is there a way to get a Charlie to be more like a Marley?

Can Self-Control Be Trained?

Once researchers began honing in on the importance of executive functioning, apparently so crucial for success in school, it was only a matter of time before they began looking for ways to instill self-control in children like Charlie. So far, they've had mixed success. To find out whether children could learn the basic tools of executive functioning in school, Cybele Raver and her colleagues selected 602 children from 35 Head Start programs to work with. Over a period of several weeks, they showed the children how to pay attention to one thing and screen out another, how to calm themselves down when they become worked up, and how to resist the temptation to call out or jump up when they should be quiet and still. They learned new simple techniques, and they got to practice the techniques. During the period of the experiment, researchers gave no special attention to those children's academic skills (beyond the regular schoolwork all the children did). In other words, if the training helped children succeed, the researchers would know that it was only because of the help they got in executive functioning, not because of any extra help in the academic topics. They also trained the children's teachers, showing them how to implement routines and be clear about rules in their classrooms, encouraging them to reward children's good behavior, and giving them strategies for redirecting children's disruptive behavior. Meanwhile, for each group of kids and teachers who learned about executive functioning, there was another group matched in age and background who did not get the special training. By the end of the year, the children who had been in the intervention groups scored higher on measures of executive functioning and effortful control. They got better, in other words, at the specific tasks included in the training (for instance, following a verbal instruction to tap a pencil while ignoring a distracting sound). However, the children didn't necessarily do better overall in school.

Other studies have shown similarly mixed results. Taken together, the research suggests that targeting one specific aspect of children's self-control—say, their ability to recall information—helps children, but in a limited way. It may be possible to teach some of the strands of behavior that are part and parcel of executive functioning, but that doesn't mean that these training techniques can transform a distracted or obstreperous child into an attentive and respectful one. Getting children to practice the individual components of executive functioning may teach them some specific behaviors, but it doesn't seem to help beyond that. Fortunately, there *are* some approaches that work well.

Two Infusion Methods for Helping Children Become Self-Directed Learners

There are a few ways to set up a classroom that help somewhat disorganized and impulsive children acquire a sense of inner control and focus. They go way beyond simple exercises or self-contained activities. In classrooms where even children like Charlie learn to wait, focus, and curb their moods, every aspect emphasizes self-regulation: the way the classroom is set up, the way teachers interact with children, and the kinds of work children are expected to engage in. Instead of isolating the skills of executive functioning and teaching them separately, these classrooms call on children to marshal their inner resources all day long. The day is infused with activities that elicit those skills.

One of these is a program called Tools of the Mind. It outlines an integrated set of interesting and rich activities for children and offers guidelines for teachers that foster self-regulation. The approach is based on the idea that children can learn self-control only when they are working on things they love to do and when some of the help is coming from peers. In other words, the model builds on two natural features of childhood: a powerful urge to be with peers and a tendency to be much more focused during intrinsically interesting activities.

In pre-K classrooms, for instance, Tools of the Mind students and teachers collaboratively select play center themes (e.g., a school in DC chose a downtown convenience store, while a school in Maine chose a lobster pound) that are particularly compelling to them. Then they create materials to bring those themes to life. Teachers provide learning activities that are related to the theme of the center. The activities tend to emphasize literacy and self-regulation—for example, children make "play plans," describing through pictures and words how they intend to structure the first few minutes of their play each day. Such planning is, after all, just a natural extension of how children spontaneously plan their own play when no adults are around: "You'll be Green Lantern, I'll shoot you down, then you'll jump up and knock me over," or "This can be the animal hospital. I'll be the vet. You bring your baby puppy and tell me he's sick." Children instantly reap the benefits of such planning, which is key to deferring rewards and modulating one's impulses. They get to build on their natural inclinations, they get more time to think about the play scenario they are so keen on, and they find themselves in an even richer, more interesting play setting. Teachers also read books to children that help them understand and engage with the themes of their play centers, again encouraging an essential academic skill that actually enhances the children's play time. Throughout all activities, students work in pairs and small groups. By the time the children get to kindergarten they still play a great deal of the time, but science, math, and literacy activities increase as well. Children write more sophisticated versions of the pre-K play plans to help them practice writing and learn to manage their time and learning goals. Common core topics are embedded in games, art projects, and dress-up and pretend play, and students continue to work in pairs. The teacher continuously emphasizes the ways in which members of the pairs can help one another: offering each other reminders, checking each other's work, and keeping track of each other's learning goals. The emphasis on interdependence and thinking things through is laced throughout the day in a myriad of small ways. For instance, each day an encoded message arrives in the classroom mailbox for the class to decode together, giving the students practice at problem-solving skills and teamwork. This is but one example of a model that emphasizes teamwork and builds on children's intrinsic interests. All of them are a great starting point for helping children like Charlie develop greater restraint and focus while learning.

The Montessori model has also had real success in helping children learn on their own and manage their impulses (see Lillard 2016). Though the name Montessori is well-known, the ideas and practices embodied by her thinking are poorly understood by most people. Like Tools of the Mind, the Montessori approach goes well beyond a set of exercises that can be added onto the existing educational plan. Instead it is meant to replace almost every aspect of conventional schools: what gets learned, how the room is set up, the role of the teacher, and even the role of the learners. Montessori classrooms are premised on two ideas which are key to helping children develop focus and self-regulation. The first idea is that children are intrinsically drawn to understanding the world around them. The Montessori approach aims to build on that intrinsic interest. The second related idea is that as long as they are offered the time, materials, and encouragement to interact with objects and people in certain ways, they will acquire information and academic skills and, most importantly, become independent learners. In other words, school learning should be a natural outgrowth of the learning children do on their own.

In both approaches, children are encouraged throughout the day to make decisions for themselves, choosing what materials to use, what they want to learn, and how to spend their time. In order for this approach to work well, the teacher must carefully, and regularly, observe the students at work. That way, when a child is ready for a new challenge, the teacher can offer one. Whole-group activities are infrequent because it is thought that such activity dilutes the child's interaction with materials.

For teachers working in most public schools in the United States, it may be very difficult to reorganize the whole learning environment and change all the educational goals already in place. But contrasting the interventions that don't seem to have much impact on self-control with these more successful approaches suggests a valuable lesson for teachers, no matter where they work. A child like Charlie might have been born with low impulse control, a short attention span, and inherent difficulty with tuning out distractions. But it took him another seven long years to practice that inattention and lack of impulse control. He had lots of opportunity to see himself as someone who got in trouble. He also went seven years without experiencing the opposite: the tremendous reward that focus and engagement bring. It would take more than thirty minutes a day for six weeks to help him overcome difficulties he was born with and had seven (or eight, nine, or ten) years to practice and amplify. The approaches that help children become more focused and able to govern themselves unfold over the whole year and permeate all parts of the school day. Some teachers who embrace these approaches might not be in a position to completely rethink their classroom setup. But they can still try to borrow as much of these ideas as possible, tweaking things so that self-generated, deeply engaging, and collaborative activities take up more rather than less of the day.

Ms. Kane felt stuck. She couldn't change everything just for Charlie. She had twenty-four kids in her classroom. And each time he called out during quiet reading, turned a chair upside down to climb on it, or began roughhousing while on line, it disrupted everyone. His outbursts and gyrations were enough to drive a teacher nutty. And among her other worries, she began to wonder whether all that unruliness could be good for Marley. They spent so much time together. What if Charlie's raucousness was contagious? Her worry about Charlie drew her to some surprises about Marley.

Mysterious Marley

Ms. Kane realized with a pit in her stomach that she hadn't been paying that much attention to Marley. She hurriedly turned back to her journal and sighed with relief. Not one note of misbehavior in all eighteen days. She saw that Marley had gotten nearly perfect scores on all the small assessments and quizzes she had given. The tightening in her stomach relaxed with relief. Marley was absolutely fine. The notes and marks showed that he was everything a teacher might ask for in a seven-year-old. He could read simple chapter books like the Magic Tree House series. He could sit quietly with a book for twenty minutes and answer questions about what he had read on a worksheet. He could add, subtract, and tell time, and he learned new concepts (fractions, for instance) at a reasonable pace. He could follow instructions and almost never seemed to have disputes with other children that spilled over into work time or called for her intervention. But that was all. Something was missing. She paused and realized that all she had was a record of his competencies. But what had Marley been up to, during all those times Charlie had been in the spotlight?

She went to the back of her notebook, where she had jotted down comments on what she had learned about each of her new students—objects or topics that grabbed their interest, quirks, funny stories, or areas of unusual accomplishment. There was nothing there for Marley. She hadn't learned anything more about him in four weeks of school, except that he was easy to have in class. But where did that leave her? Or him? As she pored back over the journal, looking for some clues, she realized that she had no idea what really mattered to Marley. What did he love; what did he veer away from? Where was his funny bone? What shut him down? And how did he see himself?

She realized that though she could easily envision Marley's calm competence, his comfort with routine, and the quiet satisfaction he took in doing things correctly, she really had no sense of what he felt or thought about various things. Charlie might drive her crazy, but at least she had a feel for who he was and what he cared about. But for Marley, not so much. Did he tolerate Charlie or really like him? Did it make him angry that he never got to be captain during the soccer games at recess? What excited him and what irked him? Of all the things he diligently did each day, which was the thing he wished he could do more of? Who was he? And was he becoming more of that person or not? What did it even mean to think about how a child became a person, anyway?

How Children Become Themselves:
The Self in Self-Control

Plato and Aristotle were the first public figures, but definitely not the last, to argue about the nature of personhood. The fundamental question was this: Are we born with a set of thoughts and characteristics that shape us (and our destiny), or are we molded through experience? Even in modern times, views on this have swung wildly from one extreme to another. During the first half of the twentieth century, John Watson (1928) and B. F. Skinner (1953) showed that children, like birds and rats, could be conditioned to be fearful or bold, obstreperous or compliant, cheerful or grouchy. If you offer a smile or small candy each time a child tries something new, according to behaviorists, she's likely to become increasingly adventurous. If you frown each time a child makes a mess, or lengthen recess each time a child cleans up, you can, supposedly, encourage tidy habits. Ironically, Freud agreed with the behaviorists in this regard. He too argued that experience mattered. It's just he focused on the long-term impact of subtle emotional interactions rather than on rewards and punishments. Behaviorists concerned themselves only with actions; Freud focused on internal feelings and thoughts.

Freud convinced generations that parents shape much of their children's personalities: how one was nursed and toilet trained and how loving or severe one's parents were determined whether a child became rigid or expansive, warm and emotionally sturdy or needy and controlling. But whether love or conditioning shapes the child, the point is that both theories point to the fact that each child's personality is sculpted through everyday experiences.

. . . whether love or conditioning shapes the child, the point is that both theories point to the fact that each child's personality has been sculpted through everyday experiences.

Some who study children reject the idea that it takes a long time and many interactions to shape a personality. Just as Aristotle set the stage for Freud and Watson, Plato introduced us to the idea that children are born with a personality already in place. In the 1960s pediatricians Stella Chess and Alexander Thomas (1965) noticed that even their three-month-old patients had distinctive personalities. Some seemed easygoing and relaxed, others fussy and tense, and still others careful and cautious. Moreover, they began to realize that the same parents, acting in roughly the same ways, often had children of wildly different temperaments. Maybe parenting didn't matter so much. Maybe babies were born with personalities. Though they built their argument on the slender basis of their own daily experiences, rigorous experimental data collected more recently have proven them right. Jerome Kagan (2009) and Nathan Fox (2001), among others, have shown that at birth babies already have clear patterns of response. When a baby sees a new toy (a mobile, for instance), her heart rate might change, she might sweat a little, and her breathing might slow down for a moment as she takes stock of this new event. Many babies will quickly take such a new experience in stride and return to their usual kicking, panting, and looking around. But not all babies. Some are so startled, their own reactions throw them out of whack. Then, because they have been startled, they become distressed, and before you know it, they are nearly inconsolable. Those reactions are strong and clear. And they are amazingly good predictors of children's future selves: how easily they'll handle new experiences, how open they'll be to encounters with others, how tough it will be for them to manage emotional peaks and valleys. To a great extent, our temperament is part of the package each of us is born with. Few would disagree with the evidence that, in Kagan's famous words, temperament casts a long shadow (Kagan and Snidman 2009). A baby who is easily startled, and reacts to any change in routine or novel experience with tension and distress, is likely to be a shy adolescent. Though a shy child might find ways to manage her reticence, she will never be the one who launches herself into a party or craves the unfamiliar. Whether a child hangs back reluctantly each morning when she gets to her classroom, or flings herself into every new situation, she will be better off if she has a strong sense of her own personality. And this all-important sense of self emerges over time.

When babies are distressed or eager to get at something, they often seem unstoppable. Their cries are desperate; they'll grab relentlessly at a toy or cookie they want; they'll persist and express themselves with abandon. But for all that noisy "selfishness," there is little evidence that they are aware of themselves as distinct individuals with particular characteristics or skills. In this way, as in a few others, Freud's scheme was right on target. They are all id (Freud's term for the part of the self we begin life with—urges and needs and a voracious drive to satisfy those needs).

But that changes quickly. If you surreptitiously put a red spot on a nine-month-old baby's nose, and show him a mirror, he will put his finger up to his nose to touch the red spot. He realizes that the person he is looking at is himself!

By the time children are two, their sense of a self has expanded exponentially. They show this firmer, fuller sense of self in all kinds of ways. They begin to use words like *I* and *me*. They talk about what they like and don't like. Ask a three- or four-year-old to tell you about herself, and usually she can. She gets the idea that there is a self to describe. She'll answer by naming the things she likes to do, her preferences, and what has happened to her. "I ride my bike. I want to eat strawberry ice cream all the time. One time my mother let me have just ice cream for dinner, and I ate a whole carton." When they are three and four they seem blithely unaware of the difference between what they want to be good at and what they are good at (for instance, the four-year-old says he can read music though what he actually does is look at a page of musical notes while enacting the hand motions of a skilled piano player). But by the time they are seven or eight many kids have a more realistic sense of their strengths and weaknesses. By the time children are seven or so, they also have some sense of what they know and what they don't know. That is, the sense of self, which begins as a cataloguing of actions and objects, becomes increasingly a portrait of the child's external and internal landscapes.

Freud aptly described the second year as the time when children acquire an ego—a sense of who they are, what they like, and what they can do. Erikson added an important nuance to Freud's conceptualization when he described this same time period as one of industry versus inferiority. Children begin to think, "I can," or "I can't." Between the ages of about four and eight, one of the most important ways children learn who they are is via other people. At home, with relatives, and in school, they hear and see people react to them, describe them, praise some behaviors, ignore others, and offer back to them a picture of who they are. William James argued that our sense of self comes from the reflections of ourselves we see in the eyes of others. (See Miller 2002 for an excellent summary of Freud, Erikson, and James.)

Meanwhile, as they busily build up subtler and more dimensional self-images, they also are creating a door between what is internal and external. By the time they are in preschool they show the first signs of a gap between their inner lives and what they reveal to others. Children as young as three posture, boast, and put on a show. They even appear to have the ability to fake it—pretend something they don't really mean or believe. In one study (Evans and Lee 2013), two- and three-year-old children were invited to play a game in which they guessed the shape of a toy that was placed on a table behind their turned backs, based on the sound it made. For instance, the researcher played a quacking noise behind the child's back, and she might guess it was a duck. After a couple of rounds of the game, the researcher told the child she needed to stop to retrieve a book from across the room and that first she would place the next toy on the table. Then she said, "But please remember, don't turn around to peek at the toy while I'm getting the book." The researcher spent the next minute rummaging in a chest with her back to the child, while a camera documented whether the child peeked. After returning, she asked if the child had peeked. Though 80 percent of the children peeked (based on the video footage), only some of those (40 percent) confessed to the peeking. And some not only kept their peeking a secret but engaged in even more elaborate trickery. When the researcher asked each child to guess the toy (without giving an auditory clue), some peekers blurted out the correct name (the researcher called these subjects "revealers"). But others feigned ignorance or guessed another toy (and were classified as "concealers"). These intriguing data suggest that by three years old, kids are developing a keen awareness of what they keep inside and what they reveal to others. In other words, when the self begins to form, so does a barrier between inner and outer, private and public. But how do they arrive at this powerful distinction between inner and outer self? One way is through play.

Children Play Their Way to a Sense of Self

Studies have shown that even two-year-olds seem to understand the special nature of pretending. Angeline Lillard watched toddlers and their mothers sit down and play tea party with a toy tea set. Mothers used exaggerated voices and facial expressions to signal that they were making believe (Lillard, Pinkham, and Smith 2011). And so did the children. This connection between pretend and the emerging sense of self has been supported by recent work by Michael Lewis and his colleagues, who have shown that the same region of the brain involved in self-recognition is also involved in various kinds of pretense and play (Lewis and Ramsey 2004). The emerging awareness of a self is key to acquiring mature forms of self-regulation.

By the time children are three or four, they not only explore dimensions of the self through pretend play but also begin using storytelling as a means of building up a sense of self. Sometimes these stories unfold casually in conversation, but given any encouragement or help at all, children can use storytelling as a powerful means of communicating to others who they feel they are and also exploring for themselves who they want to be. Take, for example, this autobiography dictated by a six-year-old to his teacher:

> When I was little, I lived at the top of a huge hill. Sometimes we used a sled to get to our car. I had a puppy named Sugar. She bit my brother's friend and we had to give her away. When I was five I won a prize for the cow pie contest. We got tickets to the Mets. I'm the fastest runner in my family.

By the time children are in kindergarten, their personalities are often on full display. Some children have a vivid sense of who they are and are happy to share that self with others. A mother told me that when her son was six the family gathered on New Year's Eve and played music so they could have a little impromptu celebration. The little boy's eighty-seven-year-old grandmother was there, as well as several aunts and uncles, his older sister and brother, and seven older cousins. The family had made a circle, and various ones took turns stepping inside the circle to dance with one another, while the outer circle called, laughed, and clapped them on. At one point the little boy, Wyatt, pushed the others who had stepped inside the circle with him back to the outside border, saying, "Move aside, people. This is my time to shine." They obliged, and he took over the dance floor for several minutes, performing an energetic mixture of break dancing and Elvis Presley moves, as if his body were being powered from within, by the music. Several years later, Wyatt's third-grade teacher asked the students to describe themselves in the shortest sentence possible. Wyatt handed in his paper. It said, "I'm all about hot pink and football." Now that's a kid who knows who he is and isn't reluctant to share it. But a child doesn't have to be as vibrant as Wyatt in order to have a strong identity.

Plenty of shy kids have a very firm sense of who they are, and they find clever ways of asserting that self, even in noisy rooms or when more dominant children steal the show. They might write or dictate stories that reveal their dreams, fears, and preoccupations. Such children often have one friend or favorite staff member (an aide, a janitor, or a food-service worker) with whom they chat about what they like to do after school or a movie or book they love. Such children often quietly and steadily persist in delving into a particular interest. Children like this don't pop out of nowhere. Instead they are likely to have had opportunities to talk, at length, with others—a parent maybe, but also a grandmother, childcare worker, or neighbor. The network of adults with whom children might, if they are lucky, communicate, explore, and strengthen their sense of identity is surprisingly wide and flexible. Shy or bold, having a clear sense of self, and the ability to share that self in a group setting, is a real asset for a child. And on this dimension, Charlie was in good shape.

Charlie may have seemed distractible and impulsive even at four. But no child is a single dimension. And at four he probably told vivid tales about his exploits and came to life, given a chance to do one of the things he loved. He wasn't one to hold back, and some of the time, this simply meant he readily shared who he was with others. On the other hand, it was hard to imagine Marley at age four telling vivid stories about what he had done or adamantly requesting the toys that would allow him to play the things he loved most.

Charlie seemed like trouble. But he had real strengths. Marley seemed like the model student. But much of who he might be remained underground. Each boy was the sum of seven years of development, seven years of particular experiences. Where did that leave Ms. Kane? Four weeks into the year, she realized that the two buddies were mirror images of one another. Perhaps there was a little too much of Charlie in the classroom, but there wasn't enough of Marley. There was a simple tool Ms. Kane could use to help both children.

A New Perspective

An extended and careful reverie, based on observation and a developmental perspective, can bring a teacher closer to figuring out how to help. Both kids needed to be understood more fully. Simply counting their outbursts and identifying their academic achievements couldn't capture all of who they were. Developmental psychology allows us to describe children, but it also gives us tools for imagining what the world might look like to each of them. Here is what such reflections might look like.

Developmental psychology allows us to describe children, but it also gives us tools for imagining what the world might look like to each of them.

Marley woke up each morning looking forward to the day. He liked his friends, he liked Ms. Kane, and he liked getting those smiley face stickers on his papers. As he stepped off the bus onto the path that led to the entrance for second graders, he remembered that his mother had given him a note to hand to Ms. Kane. He was going home with Griffin this afternoon after school. He'd give the note to his teacher right away. He didn't want any problems when it was time to get on Griffin's bus. He saw Charlie making his way toward him. He felt a nice little bubble of anticipation. Something interesting was probably about to happen. He turned and listened to Charlie, who was telling him about a cool game. He liked Charlie. When Charlie talked, Marley felt like he had just eaten a piece of chocolate: happy and energetic. But as Charlie chattered on about the levels of the game, Marley was already thinking that he should get his book from his cubby and get to the table for reading group. He knew how to tell time, and he saw that there was only one minute until Ms. Kane would ring her chime. He was a good reader, so he enjoyed reading aloud and answering the questions at the end of each section. He liked math too. Each time he solved a num-ber problem on the worksheet, he heard a nice little "ka-ching" somewhere inside his head. Correct! First reading, then math, Spanish class, and gym. Then lunch. He liked knowing the schedule. After lunch Ms. Kane would give them time to work on their papier-mâché projects; his was supposed to be about his favorite character in the book. He liked working with the wet goop. But he was having trouble thinking of what to make.

Charlie's day, from his own point of view, would look quite different. Charlie woke up each day excited for school. His openness to life's daily events probably is what gave him such apparent zest. He bounced in as if unaware of the problems he would inevitably meet as the day unfolded: kids who wouldn't want to play what he wanted to play, teachers who'd hush him, work that would seem difficult and boring, bells that would ring just when he was having fun. When he walked in each morning, he heard a lot of conversations going at once; in fact, it probably seemed so attrac-tive in so many different directions that it was a bit like arriving at a carnival—he didn't know which way to turn or what to try first. When Charlie looked around the classroom, he probably noticed all the things that invited activity—the gadgets that could be manipulated in the science corner and books whose covers just called out to be opened, but other things as well. Chairs invited pulling and tipping, hats called out to be grabbed and tried on (even if they were already on someone else's head), and all kinds of constructions were waiting to be explored (Could the tabs on the calendar be pulled off? What might fit inside the hole of the pencil sharpener?). When Ms. Kane, who always seemed less alluring than the objects and other kids in the room, rang that little bell, he felt a little thud. He knew that was the sign to take a seat at a table. But he wasn't quite ready. He'd sit down in just a minute. He just had to talk to Marley first about the game he played last night. Suddenly, just as he was launching into the good part, where he was telling Marley how he scored points, he realized Ms. Kane was talking to him, and she had that mad voice. He couldn't re-ally tell what she was saying. She was ruining his conversation with Marley. It made him mad—why did she have to cut in right then? And he also felt a little sick. Was he about to get another check mark on the Good Behavior Grid? All he had done was tell Marley a story. Why did this keep happening to him? It made him want to kick Ms. Kane in the ankle. He forgot what he had been telling Marley. And he didn't want to read anyway. He looked up at Ms. Kane's angry surprise. He *had* kicked her. He wasn't sure how that had happened. And so it went. The classroom was so cool, filled with things to watch, touch, and play with. But there were too many stupid rules and always those irritated grown-ups, who made him feel bad.

To Fix a Problem, Start by Understanding

Charlie and Marley both arrived in first grade with certain qualities that were likely to have a big impact on their lives at school. But before a teacher rushes to fix a problem, it's essential to understand just what the problem is. Most teachers, faced with these small red flags, want to make a plan and remedy things as quickly as possible. But that's a mistake. You can't fix the problem until you really understand the child—both who he is and how he got to be that way. A teacher's first step is to pay attention to her inner alarm bell, telling her to look and listen more closely. But it's not enough to look and listen. Teachers need to record their observations and impressions. Atul Gawande (2008) argues that to do their best work, doctors should count things (how many times they wash their hands, how many people get better from a certain procedure, how many conversations they have with their patients). Teachers too need to describe and record. There is a world of difference between a general impression of a kid and careful observations. Those observations can be a powerful basis for thinking through what's going on with a particular child. Which brings us to the next step: thinking about development. Children don't arrive in a classroom from nowhere. They've had years to become who they are. What, for instance, were the developmental paths that brought Charlie and Marley to their first-grade selves? Some behaviors are normal stepping-stones along the path of development. Charlie's struggle to control his impulses is fairly natural. No one is born keeping their hands to themselves or being quiet while others talk. Other characteristics reflect the specific experiences a particular child has had. Marley may have gotten lots of encouragement for behaving well and few invitations to explore what he liked and didn't like or express his inner self to others. It's essential to think about the path along which a child came to be who he or she is. Sometimes that means reeducating oneself about relevant developmental processes. How do children develop frustration tolerance, what leads to a strong sense of identity, and when is jumping up and down developmentally inappropriate? The answers are not always as obvious as one might think.

For Charlie and Marley, there was an added twist. Charlie needed a little of what Marley had, and Marley needed a little of what Charlie had. Their problems were in many ways the inverse of one another. Ms. Kane had worried that if she let them spend so much time together, it might make things worse. In fact, with just a little guidance from her, their friendship could be the solution. Charlie needed to practice self-control. Working on that with a buddy who had such good self-control would be a far more effective route than any chart with stars or jar of jellybeans. Paying attention and sticking with tasks a kid doesn't particularly like rarely works. When it does work, it's usually a short-term fix: the child gets better at keeping his voice down during math class but doesn't actually learn to become deeply immersed in work or channel his energies toward productive activity. But giving a sociable kid like Charlie the chance to try hard while working with his buddy made all the sense in the world. Meanwhile, for Marley to become slightly more expressive, more of who he was, Charlie could be a godsend. He could help Charlie learn some good habits. To do that, Marley would have to speak up a bit more. His self-control would become an interesting characteristic he could share with another kid, not just a default mode for getting through school. By sharing who he was with another kid, he would become more of that person. Ms. Kane could help both kids by getting them to help one another. She couldn't remake either of them. All she could do was guide each of them toward a slightly different developmental trajectory than the one they were on. Charlie could acquire a few new skills that would help him manage his restlessness and outbursts. Marley's interests and emotions could rise just a little more to the surface and become a stronger part of his school day. She didn't need to take any drastic measures.

On the next Monday Ms. Kane walked in and set her journal down on the desk. As she walked over to the art shelf to add some scraps of cloth she had bought at a tag sale over the weekend, she heard a loud crash. Charlie had piled several books on top of one another and then stood on top of them, trying to reach a globe placed up high, on the top of the bookshelf. The stack was wobbly, and as he stretched to grab the globe, the pile toppled over and he fell. Marley was standing nearby quietly, watching. He seemed amused but also startled. He wouldn't have abandoned Charlie in a moment like that. But he didn't want to be part of the trouble either. It was a great moment for Ms. Kane to step in and help the boys begin forging a new kind of partnership. At break time, she went over to the two boys as they huddled to look at a new book Charlie had brought in about superheroes. Leaning down quietly, she said, "I've noticed you two have a lot of the same interests. I have an idea that you will really work well together. Here's what we'll do. You two will be a team during reading, math and our history projects. You'll take turns being in charge of the team work. And every Friday you'll have a little time to sit down with a snack, and give each other some feedback about how the teamwork went. . . ."

CHAPTER SEVEN

Wrong School for Audrey?

———◆———

Poverty ★ Cognition: Part Three ★ Literacy

AUDREY SAT DOWN to have breakfast with her former professor. She was visiting her alma mater on the East Coast, one year after graduation, and a mere three weeks since she had finished her first year of teaching kindergarten. It would be her last. At least at that school.

Audrey had studied education while in college and had accepted a job at an elementary school in Cincinnati against the advice of her professor, who had said, "The school promotes an awfully rigid approach. I don't know if that will suit someone with your ideas, your training, and your personality." But Audrey was drawn to it anyway. She knew the school had a reputation for being somewhat formulaic; all teachers were expected to adhere to specific methods, children wore uniforms, and supervision was heavy. But Audrey didn't want to teach in a cushy suburb like the one where she had grown up. White and middle-class, she was eager to dive into a different kind of community. What she wanted most was to be part of a school that gave minority and low-income children a chance to do well. Cincinnati was packed with low-income residents. The children, most of whom were black in this particular neighborhood, were stuck in decrepit schools with inadequate space, patched windows, and bleak, blank walls. For the most part, the schools were also understaffed by teachers who received little professional support for their work. Yet the city was brimming with interesting communities of people, activism, a vibrant mix of old and new food, entertainment, politics, and culture. It seemed like just the place to be. And though the school's philosophy might appear formulaic to Audrey's college professor, to Audrey the school merely seemed committed to doing things differently. It was a charter school, part of a larger network. The whole network had outlined a wide range of practices that the staff felt sure would be particularly good for children who started kindergarten already at a disadvantage.

The Iron Grip of Poverty

Imagine walking into the nursery of an obstetrics ward and looking at all the new baby boys and girls lying in their bassinets, tightly swaddled. If someone asked you what single piece of information would be most helpful in order to predict which of those babies would be doing well in school by third grade, and which would be falling behind, what would you say? Many people assume the answer is IQ (it can be tested in infancy and is remarkably accurate and stable). But they are wrong. Ever since Malcolm Gladwell wrote *Outliers*, people have been inclined to believe that quirky twists of fate, like the baby's birth month, provide strangely useful information about a child's future prospects. But that's not true either. The single most useful piece of information is, sadly, the baby's parents' income level. Children who are born into poverty, in our country, are very likely to struggle in school by third grade (Shonkoff and Phillips 2000, Burchinal et al. 2000). We know some, but not all, of the reasons for this.

The best-known reason is the mighty yet somewhat mysterious connection between poverty and language. Psychologists Hart and Risley (1995) studied forty-two families from the time the children were nine months old until they were three years old and then tracked the children through third grade. Some families were what they called "talkative." They used lots of words to say all kinds of things (to offer practical information to one another, chitchat, entertain, and inform). Other families were what the researchers labeled taciturn. They tended to talk sparingly, only when absolutely necessary, mostly for practical purposes, and they relied on a bare-bones vocabulary. On average young children hear about 1,500 words an hour, which supports the explosion of word learning they must accomplish. But that average is deceptive, because there is so much variation between families. The children of professional, educated parents hear about 2,100 words an hour, while children from families on welfare hear about 600 words an hour. By four, children of professional talkative families have heard 48 million words. Children from welfare taciturn families have heard 13 million words.

Why would the amount of talk children hear at home determine their chance of success at school? The reasons begin to emerge when you take a closer look at the data. It turns out that the *amount* of talk children hear at home is linked to the *kind* of talk they hear. Children who hear minimal language at home are exposed, for the most part, to what Hart and Risley call "business talk": brief commands ("Eat your cereal" or "Don't do that"), practical information ("We're having pizza" or "Your shoes are over there"), and simple direct questions ("Did you wash your face?"). Children who grow up in wordier families hear something different, what Hart and Risley call extra talk. Their parents use a more varied vocabulary for a wider range of purposes: to describe ("Look at how dark that cloud is," "That story made me really sad," and "You bounce like a rubber ball"), to ask questions that go beyond the immediate situation ("Whom did you see on the playground?" and "Did you think that was Grandpa coming in last night?"), and to speculate ("If you keep pouring water in there, I think it's going to turn to mush"). The amount of extra talk a child hears at three has a .77 correlation with scores on the Peabody Picture Vocabulary Test at third grade (a widely used and very dependable measure of a child's school success). We know that the amount and types of talk a child hears at home play a huge role in academic success. But the reasons why poorer children hear less language at home is not yet fully clear to researchers.

In recent years, researchers have discovered that children who face crises on a daily basis develop coping strategies that they carry with them into the classroom. Poverty brings with it a particular set of these frequent crises.

Poverty shapes children in other ways as well. In recent years, researchers have discovered that children who face crises on a daily basis develop coping strategies that they carry with them into the classroom. Poverty brings with it a particular set of these frequent crises. Children might not know where they will sleep on any given night or whether there will be enough food for them that day, and they frequently confront the risk of neighborhood violence. Children who are poor and non-white confront the threats of racism and marginalization on a daily basis as well. Children who live with these stressors often develop coping strategies that help them manage uncertainty, bigotry, violence, and physical discomfort. But those maneuvers are not likely to help them when they are sitting at a table in school, trying to solve math problems. And yet, by the time such children are seven, the coping strategies they've developed at home are already pretty well set, which puts them at a big disadvantage when it comes to navigating a classroom. A child who has learned, through experience, to tense up, to either flee or fight when faced with any hint that something is scary or threatening, might be at an advantage when walking home on a dangerous street. But neither fleeing nor fighting is helpful when the thing scaring you is a math problem.

It made sense to Audrey, when she was looking for her first teaching job, to pick a school that was very deliberate in its approach to educating kids from low-income backgrounds. She had taken college courses on poverty, racism, and the politics of education. From everything she had learned, helping a poor child succeed in school was a huge challenge and called for major shifts in conventional ideas about education. She was ready to accept the idea that the teaching methods that had worked for her (a white girl with professional parents who had grown up in a middle-class white neighborhood) would not necessarily help a poor black child from a poor city with palpable racial tensions.

When she went for her interview at the school to which she was applying, she noticed all of the children were in uniforms. She asked why that was so, and the teacher whose class she had visited said, "Well, it is one way of helping them have a school identity, a sense that we are all part of a big family here at school, a little different than our homes. It makes everyone feel like they are part of the team. And . . . ," he added, "it also discourages them from competing about clothes; kids who are poor don't have to be so worried that they will look shabby at school, and the girls don't have to spend so much time trying to outdo one another. It's an equalizer." Audrey liked that. It showed her that the school was really thinking about its particular students.

On that same tour, she also noticed how peaceful things seemed in the hallways. She was impressed. During her job search, she had visited some other schools in Cincinnati, where there had been a constant din and a sense of barely controlled chaos most of the time. She hadn't liked the feeling she'd gotten in those buildings. It seemed unpleasant, and she could only imagine how unpleasant or scary it might be to a five-year-old. When she entered this building, and saw children all dressed the same, walking to the cafeteria in a quiet, orderly line, she had sighed with relief. She could see herself working here. And so when they offered her the job, she took it. She understood her professor's concerns, but she thought to herself, "Professor Moore lives in an ivory tower. She doesn't understand what these particular kids need." Audrey felt really excited about this next chapter of her life.

In mid-August she moved into her new apartment and began her orientation. There were eight other teaching assistants who would begin when she did. Many were recent college graduates, but some already had a master's degree as well as a few years of teaching experience. She noticed that more than a third of the head teachers were also new—not necessarily young or new to teaching, just new to this school. That seemed a bit odd, but maybe a lot of older teachers had just retired, she thought. She was relieved that they all would spend a full two weeks preparing together.

During those first days she and the other new teachers were given guidelines for everything: They were told what the schedule should be in their classroom each day, how to introduce various lessons, and how to give help to individual students. They went over a range of clearly described techniques for refocusing children, setting limits, giving consequences, and rewarding good behavior. She was a bit thrown by how much everything she was learning felt like it came from one big instructor's manual. There was a specification for almost everything. But she was also grateful. Up until then, her only classroom experience had been as a student teacher, filling a practicum requirement during college. What did she know about how to handle a lively group of five-year-olds?

When her twenty-six new students arrived on August 29, she was unexpectedly nervous. She hadn't anticipated what a big deal it would feel like to come face-to-face with all those small girls and boys. These twenty-six kids, in their bright uniforms, carrying backpacks and staring at her with undisguised curiosity, would be her constant companions for more than six hours a day, all year long. And it wasn't as if they were just twenty-six individuals. It felt like a huge crowd, pulsing with a life of its own, like some large sea creature.

When she looked closely at each face, and shook their small warm hands, she got her first glimmers of their personalities. A little girl greeted her with an easy, charming smile, her body relaxed and bouncy; she seemed confident. One little boy looked at her inscrutably, his face tense and his gait stiff. He seemed angry, or terrified, she couldn't tell which, and that unnerved her. Another little boy started talking to her midsentence, as if he had already been in a conversation with her. He didn't seem to realize that they had never met, that she was someone new. That shook her a little too. But when she stepped up to the front of the class to begin, all those first impressions evaporated. They were once again just a big pulsing mob, on the verge, maybe, of anarchy. Thank god she had a script to follow.

Within just a few days, Audrey had shed the daily sense of terror that the group might erupt into chaos. Her fear that she was constantly on the edge of a disaster or about to screw up faded a little. The ironclad routines and the carefully spelled-out lessons provided by the administration meant that she and the children soon knew the ropes. Each day the children began by singing the school song using the hand motions they had easily learned. Then they quickly moved on to a variety of academic tasks (she and the other new teachers had been told, during orientation, not to give the kids enough time to lapse into silliness between activities, but to keep them on a tight schedule).

John Watson's Return

Every day, Audrey or her head teacher, Mr. Miller, started each lesson the same way: deliver instructions, go over the rules of conduct for the task, explicitly state the learning goal of the activity, and then make sure the children understood what they should do. Often these instructions and procedures were also projected onto a white screen with peppy colored images and simple words, so the children knew exactly what was expected of them and could begin to relate what the teachers said out loud with the written symbols and words. The children loved the morning song, and for the most part, they seemed ready and willing to follow the instructions they heard each morning. But that didn't mean everything was smooth sailing. Plenty of the kids wiggled in their designated spots, became distracted during the instruction phase, or began looking around at other children when they were supposed to be tracing letters on a sheet. Sometimes two children surreptitiously began talking or fooling around, and before Audrey knew it, they were laughing loudly or horsing around. At least two or three times a day these quiet little dances and wriggles erupted into fights. But even then, Audrey had been given very clear tools for handling the disruptions.

When she first practiced the self-control tools she learned during orientation, she was really impressed. She knew, from college, that many of the children she'd be working with would arrive at school with no clue about waiting their turns, calming themselves down, or refocusing after an interruption. She had also read a book by Lisa Delpit called *Other People's Children* (2006). She had been jolted by Delpit's claim that many of the methods used by white middle-class teachers just didn't match the understandings and expectations of children growing up in communities different from their own. The example that really rang a bell was Delpit's description of progressive teachers who tended to use indirect requests, which seemed to them to be friendly and gentle, like, "Would everyone like to put away their chairs now?" Delpit argued that children who came from traditional black southern neighborhoods heard that phrase completely differently than white children—not as a coded command, but as a genuine question. Their internal answer to what sounded to them like a genuine question was, naturally enough, "No, I wouldn't like to." They didn't catch the implicit command, and when they didn't move the chair, the teacher thought they were being uncooperative or disobedient. Nor was this only a matter of race or class. Audrey remembered her own father saying that when he was a little boy in a posh private school for white children in New York City, a teacher had said to him, "Peter, you need to get ahold of yourself." But Peter had no idea how to get ahold of himself. He didn't even know what that meant. So hearing that scornful admonishment made him feel bad and left him just as unsuccessful in the classroom as before. Audrey thought the same might often be true of children who weren't behaving because they didn't understand the rules they were supposed to follow. So Audrey was eager to offer her young students more explicit guidance when they got a little unruly.

One of the interesting techniques she learned went like this: When a student seemed so overcome with emotion that he or she could no longer concentrate, she would bring the child over to the take-five corner, a quiet corner of the room surrounded on three sides by low bookshelves and covered with a brightly colored carpet. There she would invite the overexcited five-year-old to sit on his or her bottom on a pillow and choose one of three or four objects from a basket (a stuffed teddy bear, a brightly colored plastic set of interconnected tubes, a small patterned bean bag and a Rubik's Cube). Then, as the child watched, Audrey would flip over a large plastic four-minute timer, smile, and leave the child to hold onto his or her chosen comfort item, while waiting for the sand in the timer to sprinkle down to the bottom. After four minutes, Audrey would come back and hand the child a clipboard on which was clipped a piece of paper with wide lines, made for kids who were just learning how to write. On the sheet were three statements: "Before I felt ___. Then I ___. Now I feel ___." Most of Audrey's students couldn't write yet, so she took dictation. Children were supposed to say things like, "Before I felt mad. Then I held the teddy bear. Now I feel happy." The whole exchange was supposed to require about five minutes of the child's time and two minutes of Audrey's time. The workshop leaders had explained that by going through these steps each time, the kids finally had the opportunity to learn techniques that perhaps other children had acquired at home, but these children had not. Rather than floundering on their own to "get ahold of themselves," they were practicing good ways to manage their feelings. Nothing about it was vague. While the children were calming down, they were also learning, very explicitly, the steps required to shake off a bad feeling.

To Audrey, it was a relief to know just what to do each time a kid acted out. Most of the kids, most of the time, seemed equally relieved. The steps were straightforward and clear. When she watched them go through the sequence, it seemed as if the concentration it took to choose the toy, watch the timer, and answer the questions gave most of them the chance to unwind and settle down.

By the second week Audrey felt like she had been there a long time. It wasn't as if she had everything worked out. In fact she was still exhausted by the intensity of the pace and all the pieces of the day that were new to her. But she felt as if she had known these particular children forever; they were part of her consciousness from the moment she woke up until the moment she fell asleep. Sometimes she dreamed about them. She already had a kind of Spidey sense about which children were likely to liven up a particular activity and which kid might get thrown out of whack by a change in the routine. She definitely knew, she realized somewhat guiltily, whom she gravitated toward, not to mention which kids gave her a sick sense of dread.

The children that left her most uneasy were the ones who not only got in trouble several times a day, but seemed shocked and miserable each time they were sent over to the take-five corner or lost a marble. On the second day of the year, Mr. Miller had brought out a big glass mason jar. The kids had watched with interest. He'd held the jar up and said to the group, "Do you know what this is for?" A few kids had raised their hands. "It's a jar. Pickles." "It's for fish." "I know, I know; you are gonna put candy in it for us." Mr. Miller had said, "No. But good guesses. This jar is a party jar. Every time I catch one of you being kind, or listening well, I'll put a marble in it. When the jar is full up, we can have a party. But if one of you misbehaves, I'll take a marble out. So you really need to listen to our instructions, sit still, and follow the rules. Remember, hands glued together, eyes on the teacher!" He had showed them what it looked like to glue your hands together. The kids had nodded solemnly, watching as Mr. Miller put the jar high up on a shelf behind his desk, where all the kids could see it but none could reach it. He had dropped three bright marbles into the jar, saying, "These are because you've made such a good start to the year. This morning I noticed you all put your things away neatly in your classroom cubby, you all sat down on the carpet as soon as I rang my chime, and you are listening very, very well!" Less than a moment later, a little boy named Derek had shouted out angrily to another child who was sitting next to him on the carpet, "Hey, Richie. Stop it. Stop pushing me." Derek had shoved Richie away from him. Mr. Miller had quietly and quickly taken a marble out of the jar, as all of the children had watched with dismay.

In college Audrey took Psychology 101. She learned all about Pavlov's experiments, showing that by pairing a specific sound or sight with some other sound or sight, or with a particular experience or behavior, you could get a dog, a rat, and even a person to associate those two things every time. If, for instance, you blow a whistle every time you give the person a snack, then the person is likely to feel hungry or water at the mouth every time she hears a whistle, even when no food is around. Imagine, instead, you give your subject a slight shock each time she hears the whistle. Now, instead of salivating, your subject is likely to cower when you blow the whistle. Behaviorism also predicts that when you reward certain behaviors, you will increase them, and when you punish a behavior, you can decrease it. Imagine, say, that every time you raise your voice, people around you fall silent and let you finish. When you speak quietly, no one listens. A behaviorist would predict that over time the subtle reward for shouting (compliance from others) will encourage you to shout more often. The lack of reward you get for speaking in a quiet tone will lead that quieter voice to disappear over time. The basic idea of the theory goes like this: we can't ever know what's really going on in someone else's mind, but we can predict what she'll do. In thousands of experiments, researchers have shown that you can shape a person's behavior through small rewards and punishments associated with simple behaviors. Reward a good behavior, and the person will engage in the behavior again. Stop rewarding, and the target behavior will dwindle and disappear.

Among other phenomena, behaviorism has been used to explain how and why children acquire habits, knowledge, and characteristics as they grow. John Watson, the father of American behaviorism, wrote a guide just for parents (Watson 1932). The gist of the book is that children are born with a few basic instincts and responses (for example, the fear of loud sounds and loss of support, as well as the need for comfort and food). By pairing various stimuli with those basic responses, the growing child builds up a huge and complex set of associations that comprise the self. Behaviorism views development as a steady increase in associations; the twenty-three-year-old is simply the sum of all the rewards and punishments that person has experienced over his or her lifetime.

Most people don't think much about whether they subscribe to the theory of behaviorism or not. But nearly everyone uses the theory in their daily lives, especially parents and teachers. Probably every teacher can think of a recent time when he or she gave a student a smiley face on a piece of work, an extra five minutes at recess, an A, or a "good job" for lining up quickly, solving a sheet of math problems, or helping another child. You're rewarding students for good behavior, conditioning them to repeat that behavior next time. It's behaviorism in practice. Sometimes teachers shape children's behavior using a subtler kind of conditioning: a teacher scolds the children when they roughhouse and stops scolding when they refrain from rough-housing. The teacher doesn't intend this; it just happens. Nevertheless, it's a power-ful way of molding children's behavior. The removal of an unpleasant consequence can be just as effective as the introduction of a pleasant one or a punishment. For instance, consider a teacher who yells when her students leave their books on the floor. If for some reason the children begin putting away their books and, as a result, no longer hear the unpleasant yelling, this is called negative reinforcement. It's not at all the same thing as punishment. In fact, research has consistently shown that punishments, which are so often used in schools, are the least effective way to shape a child's behavior. Taking five minutes away from recess every time a child loses his temper does very little to change a child's behavior in the long run (see Patricia Miller 2002).

But behaviorism offers something beyond a set of techniques for modifying a child's actions. It rests on a powerful core assumption about children: development is nothing more than the steady accumulation of learned behaviors. That idea, taken seriously, suggests that education is simply the process of rewarding the behaviors you want children to learn—knowledge and skills as well as habits and actions—and ignoring or punishing the ones you want to rid them of. A true behaviorist sees no difference between this kind of learning, which is visible, and any internal transfor-mation that might occur beneath the surface over a long period of time. When Mr. Miller pulled out the jar and the marbles, Audrey thought to herself, "So that's what behaviorism looks like. Now I get it." It might, she thought, train Derek not to shove during group time. But would it help him grow into a less angry person or channel his anger in a more interesting or productive way? She had her doubts.

In addition to the marble jar, there were a lot of other small routines sprinkled throughout the day. Some of the rituals seemed to offer the children limitless satis-faction. They loved the different songs used at various junctures: the one to begin the day, a different one, all about figuring, which they sang right before math, and yet another one, about settling down, which they sang after recess. Each song was accompanied by its own little routine of hand gestures, and the better the kids got at the songs, the more satisfaction they seemed to feel in the whole thing.

Why *did* the children like all of those small routines, and why had the school put so many into the schedule? When Audrey mused out loud one day about it at lunch, a teacher who planned to retire that spring said, with tired certainty, "Kids love rou-tine. They find it comforting." But that is only a small part of it. A look at research on children's thinking points to a more profound explanation.

Routines: A Cognitive Foundation

In the mid 1970s, Katherine Nelson (1998) was interested in research on the development of children's memory. All of the studies she was reading as a young scientist suggested that under the age of about five, kids had poor memories. When they heard a list of words or numbers, they were unable to repeat them back to an experimenter, even just a few moments after they heard them. They couldn't recall instructions. In fact, they couldn't even seem to tell a researcher what they had done in preschool the day before. The prevailing explanation was that memory span grows with age, and the children just didn't have enough bandwidth, at ages three and four, to recall much of anything. This made no sense to Nelson. She had a hunch that the children's difficulty revealed something much more important than small bandwidth. Perhaps researchers were asking children the wrong questions.

To test memory, researchers had asked children questions that seemed perfectly straightforward, like, "What did you eat for breakfast this morning?" Kids would stare at them blankly, shrug, or offer a tentative partial answer (often wrong, when checked against their mother's or father's report). Nelson thought it was possible that before children can recall specific memories from their past (what they ate that particular morning), they first develop a more general outline of their experiences. And so, she and her students made a very small change in the question. They began asking three-year-olds: "What do you usually have for breakfast (or lunch or dinner)? What do you do at a birthday party, during bath-time, or at preschool?" Lo and behold, asked this way, even three-year-olds readily answered: "I eat oatmeal. And sometimes I have a banana. Then Mommy lets me drink some orange juice, if I want it." Children did remember their experiences but not in terms of specific descriptions for specific events. Instead, they seemed to remember a general script for an event which they had experienced routinely.

The ramifications of her studies were huge. First, the data showed that our ideas about children's abilities are often a product of what we ask them to do rather than what they *can* do, or *would* do, given other questions and tasks. Secondly, Nelson's studies proved that children know and remember a lot about their everyday lives. Third, and perhaps most important, the studies suggested something quite profound about the nature of knowledge itself: children organize their knowledge around the activities and goals that are meaningful to them and the other people with whom they live. Nelson argued that children represent knowledge in terms of scripts, and that these scripts have a stable structure: the main purpose or goal of the activity (breakfast, bath time, and so on), the key events (first I have oatmeal; then I have juice), the characters (me and Mommy), and the parts that might vary from time to time (sometimes I have a banana). These scripts set the stage for further knowledge.

Nelson predicted that once children had acquired a clear and firm sense of the various scripts representing their daily experiences, they would be able to recall specific instances from that script (what they had for breakfast the day of the storm, on Christmas morning, or today). In other words, a general understanding of the basic routines of life laid down the groundwork for the more particular kinds of thinking and memory that came a little later. For instance, children might learn more abstract concepts, like furniture, or tools, by first learning the script for helping Mommy or Daddy around the house. Audrey realized that it wasn't just emotionally comforting for the children to participate in all the daily rituals and routines. It provided them with the kinds of information on which they could hang new knowledge. Giving them a way to script the day would allow them to notice variations, commonalities, and patterns. If scripts were the basic building blocks to thinking, then routines would be intellectually as well as emotionally helpful. But maybe there was a downside.

A few children, like Derek, haunted Audrey. He listened when she or Mr. Miller reminded the children of rules or set forth a new one. But he couldn't follow them. And each time his behavior led to some form of punishment, he just got sadder and angrier. Audrey wondered whether five-year-olds were meant to sit so still and keep their eyes on the teacher with their hands glued together. That was the one that bothered her most. Is that what five-year-olds should be doing with their hands?

Audrey kept thinking back to Jean Piaget's discovery that long before children can sit quietly and simply think about something (numbers, stories, how cells divide, what it means to be fair, and so on), they think with their bodies. In fact new research suggests that we continue to think with our bodies long after we've left the dress-up corner and block area behind. A great deal of current research looks at what is known as embodied cognition—the ways in which we gesture, move our heads, walk, and

Imagine how crucial embodied cognition is for children who don't yet have an interest or competence in thinking things through while sitting quietly at a desk. It's not just that they are fidgety or lack focus. They need to use their bodies in order to think.

experience sensations as a critical part of thinking (Smith and Gasser 2005, Shapiro 2010). Imagine how crucial embodied cognition is for children who don't yet have an interest or competence in thinking things through while sitting quietly at a desk. It's not just that they are fidgety or lack focus. They need to use their bodies *in order* to think.

If you doubt this, conjure up the image of a toddler as she goes about her daily life. There are two things you can count on: (1) she will be curious about almost everything new she encounters, and (2) she will taste, touch, kick, open, or tap as a way of finding out about anything that piques her curiosity. The reason children learn so much during the first few years of life (when you think about it, far more than they will probably ever learn again) is because they are so attentive to new information and wired to study whatever surprises them. They are also intrepid explorers. This is why psychologist Jerome Kagan has said that if you put babies in a new room, 90 percent of them will spend about twenty seconds scanning the situation and then begin avidly exploring it. At first, at least, these explorations are almost completely physical. They quickly acquire a formidable new tool for exploration: questions. However, they continue to use their bodies to learn. Just imagine a five-year-old at the sand table or outside in a playground that contains dirt and shrubs. She'll dig, pile, pour, and pull. Each time, she'll be testing a hypothesis about how the world works. As far as Audrey was concerned, when their hands were stilled, so were their minds.

Audrey began to realize she hated telling children to glue their hands together. And some kids, like Derek, just couldn't. He needed his hands to express himself, to distract himself, to calm himself. And by demanding he keep them clasped, she was pushing him into trouble, again and again. As the weeks unfolded, she felt queasier and queasier about punishing kids for acting like five-year-olds. When she opened her old textbook from college, she saw that research has shown that, as they get older, most children think less with their bodies and more with the symbols and words in their minds. It might make sense for an eleven-year-old to sit quietly and think about a number line. But a five-year-old really can't do it without moving around. An eight-year-old can talk about how frustrated she is that her friend keeps teasing her, whereas a five-year-old is just as likely to jump up and down, screw her face up with anger, and yes, even, push. It's not bad. It's not unnatural. It's young. By the same token, it's natural for adults to encourage children to become more self-contained. But children don't go from experiencing the world through their bodies to contemplating the world with their minds overnight. That shift is slow and gradual. Helping a child along the path from action as a means of thinking to reflective contemplation is a very different enterprise from training him to obey.

Audrey began to think it might help to encourage children like Derek to *use* their bodies, rather than suppress them, during times of excitement. What if there were a corner of the room where he could act out his emotions in mime or make some vivid drawings or a sculpture of his thoughts? What if that offered him a midway point between learning with his body and reflecting from a chair in words and symbols? Developmental psychologists would describe such drawings or miming as enactive symbolization, meaning when children draw images or use words that are, however indirectly, similar to the words and feelings they are trying to capture. Audrey pursued this idea a little further. What if she encouraged Derek to make up stories that allowed him to express his wish for revenge and turn his turbulent impulses into good fiction for the other children to read?

Audrey suggested as much to her head teacher, Mr. Miller. He was alarmed. "That just gives them the message it's OK to feel angry. I think it will just egg Derek on if he writes poems about fighting or makes pictures of shouting at people." Audrey didn't say much. She was so new to this. But she had the feeling that even if they could force or train a child like Derek to keep his hands glued together, it wouldn't help him figure out how to have the angry feelings without disrupting the group or hurting the person toward whom he felt angry. And was it really not OK for a five-year-old to feel angry sometimes? Wasn't it reasonable that spending the whole day in a group of other five-year-olds, away from his family, trying to do things that didn't come all that naturally to him might make him a bit emotional and squirmy?

It wasn't just the hands-glued-together rule that bothered her, either. Early on, the children's uniforms had been such a cheerful sign of the school's unity. The bright orange was a vivid visual clue that the kids could leave various problems (like poverty and erratic home lives) at home. Here, they wore the same uniform, they were part of a community, and their commonalities were greater than their differences. But after a few weeks the bright orange sweatshirts had begun to make her wince. It began one Monday morning, in the sixth week of school. During their morning share time, a little girl named Iris announced, "My dad and me, we went to see my uncle Norm this weekend. He was wearing the same school uniform as us!"

Audrey was confused. "Your uncle Norm is a student here?"

Iris gave Audrey the look kids have when they can't believe how clueless you are. "Uncle Norm's in jail. But he wears an orange suit, just like me!"

Audrey's stomach clenched. It had never occurred to her that for some of these children, the color of their school uniform was also the color worn by relatives who were incarcerated in the nearby prison.

The Home–School Connection

Children in China share differently than children in Canada, and children in Copenhagen have skills that children in San Francisco do not. But there's one thing that is true of children everywhere: the more they feel that their school connects to their lives at home, the better they like school and the more they get out of it. What kind of connections does that entail? Here are a few examples. Children are natural storytellers (Engel 1995). By the time they are two they can refer to something from the past and put together fledgling stories. They also listen to stories—not just the ones in books, but the small casual stories they hear in everyday conversations. Sometimes people tell them stories ("Remember yesterday, when you ate the whole cupcake? It was all over your face, right? And then Snoopy licked it off your chin. That was funny, right?"). But often they merely overhear the stories adults are sharing with one another. ("This morning at work, I had such a fight with my officemate. She keeps shouting when she's making calls. And I was like, 'Either you lower your voice, or I'm gonna ask for a new officemate.' And she was like, 'I'm not shouting. No one else ever complains about my voice.'") Needless to say, the stories children hear in one community may differ quite a bit from the stories children hear in another community.

All the stories children hear help them learn how to tell their own stories. Once they get to school, the way that their teachers and the other kids respond to their stories helps them build up their own repertoire of narrative skills.

All the stories children hear help them learn how to tell their own stories. Once they get to school, the way that their teachers and the other kids respond to their stories helps them build up their own repertoire of narrative skills. But some children learn one style of storytelling at home, only to find that the teachers and other children at their school tell a very different kind of story, for a very different purpose. When their stories are overlooked, or constantly corrected by teachers at school, they lose out in two ways. First, they become less eager to tell stories and less confident about the value of their stories. Secondly, they miss out on the opportunity to receive the kind of feedback that children use to get better at storytelling.

Continuity between home and school helps in another way. When parents want the same things for their children that the school wants, children get more out of their educational experience. In the most famous study looking at home-school relations, Harold Stevenson and Shin-ying Lee compared children in three cultures: China, Japan, and the United States (Stevenson et al. 1990). In particular, they wanted to find out why children in China and Japan did so much better on international assessments of reading and math by the end of elementary school. First they ruled out the possibility that the Japanese and Chinese children were simply smarter or intrinsically better at those particular activities; there was no difference between the children when they entered school. But by fifth grade, the Chinese and Japanese children were more skilled on a whole host of tests. Why would this be? It turned out that one of the biggest differences between the Asian schools and the ones in the United States was the attitude parents had about school. The families in China and Japan felt closely in synch with the goals and aims of their children's schools; they liked the traditions at the schools, they agreed with the things the schools cared about, and they felt that at home they should build on whatever the schools were trying to teach their children.

Audrey began to make an informal count of the number of students who mentioned a relative who had been, or was currently, in jail. It turned out there were a lot of them—more than 25 percent by her count. What did it feel like to wear clothes that, to them, resembled prison uniforms? What was it like for parents to send their children to school each day wearing a miniature version of what they had seen their brothers, aunts, and cousins forced to wear in jail? Could parents feel that the school was a welcoming place that would help their children thrive, if the children were dressed like inmates? One teacher argued that the orange uniforms were fine; why should the children associate the orange sweatshirts with jail clothes? But that teacher wasn't remembering that even very young children are sponges when it comes to absorbing messages about the attitudes and values of those around them. And the message those students were likely to hear was that their school knew very little about their lives at home and didn't care if the orange clothes evoked thoughts of their relatives in prison.

Audrey kept telling herself that even though there were things that made her uncomfortable about the school, her kids were terrific and, equally important, the methods were paying off. After all, she saw the test results from last year's kindergarten class. The children now in first grade were doing quite well on various assessments of their reading. They had a good grasp of beginning phonics, they recognized a large number of words by sight, and they seemed pretty skilled when it came to things like identifying syllables, recognizing compound words, and mastering other building blocks of literacy.

Then, in early February, she sat down with a small group of the kids for a read-aloud session. She had chosen a story from a collection that the teachers had been told was appropriate for the reading level of their highest-performing kids. It was a story about a kitten called Mittens. For a Halloween story, it was strangely cheerful and calming. The children sat down on the floor, each on one of the brightly colored squares that signified a sitting spot. She read the first page and then asked each of the seven children, in turn, to read one of the pages aloud. As one began pronouncing the words, Audrey looked around at the other six children. One had already turned to the last page. Two were looking at each other, making faces. Two were watching a group of children at another table, who were being chastised for not listening to the instructions. The one who was carefully sounding out the words, following along with her finger, was concentrating mightily. But not on the story—just on the words. Audrey realized that though all the emphasis on skills had helped the kids learn to read, they didn't *like* to read. As her mind scanned the past few weeks, she realized she'd never seen a child, even in this top group, pick up a book on his or her own or ask to read during their fifteen minutes of free-choice time.

Literacy from A to Z

As every elementary school teacher knows, the battle over how best to teach reading rages on. Some are committed to the power of a phonics approach: help a child break down the code of the written word into its symbols, sounds, and rules, and he'll be able to read anything. Others are just as adamant about the importance of having children read full sentences and stories from the beginning, learn to guess as they go along, recognize sight words, and figure out sentences by their context. The fight between advocates of whole language and phonics has kept many educational journals afloat for years. But psychologists who have watched children learn to read know that the truth is messier, and yet simpler, than devotees of a particular method would have you believe. The truth is that children begin laying the groundwork for literacy when they are still babies. Learning to talk is the first step. But it's not the only way they prepare to be readers. They also learn about the rules of conversation and grammar. They do this via all manner of simple games they play with their caregivers; patty-cake, trot trot to Boston, and peekaboo are just three examples from the United States. As Jerome Bruner first showed, those games teach children how to take turns but also about the structure of thinking and writing: the idea of sequence, resolution, variation, and so on. Meanwhile, very young children are preparing to be readers in another way, and it's not by memorizing the alphabet, as some eager young parents believe. It's by listening to their parents, siblings, cousins, and neighbors tell stories and by telling their own.

Early on, their narratives are extremely rudimentary, at least from a literary perspective. At first children may only offer the kernel of a story about something that has happened to them (Engel 1995). A toddler says, "My balloon," and her father responds, "Yes, you had that cool balloon. What happened to it?" The toddler replies, "Bye-bye," and the father says, "You said, 'Bye-bye,' didn't you? Because you let go, didn't you? Oh well."

Some kids are lucky enough to have family members who join in, elaborating the kernel, asking questions that invite them to expand their tales. In this example, the father embeds his child's two-word starter in several more complex sentences. This elaboration leads his daughter to add her own detail: She said, "Bye-bye," because the balloon got away. The father's response adds useful information about what makes a good description (put your story in the past tense, provide details, offer some evaluation, and add some dramatic action). By the end of this brief exchange, they have reminisced about a shared experience and the little girl has acquired some new conversational techniques. Researchers who have recorded children in their homes have discovered that most parents are natural language guides (Greenfield 1984). These parents provide all kinds of help without any specific pedagogical motive; they simply want to talk, exchanging ideas and sharing experiences with someone they care about. Although casual, such collaborations are invaluable to children. Children who have a lot of conversations at home learn to read more easily when they get to school. And children who read more easily like reading better and read more often.

Children's first stories are about their real experiences. But by the time they are three, they also tell made-up stories. Here too, the more they are encouraged to share their narratives, the stronger their literacy skills will be farther down the road. After all, a child who can recognize the sound of every letter or can read sentences smoothly by the time he is six would be at a total loss, in terms of reading, if he had no sense of plot, character, and the importance of sequence. But conversations are also a powerful way of letting children learn about the world they cannot touch, bang, taste, or take apart. Conversations provide a first path into another crucial aspect of literacy. They provide children with a way to learn about the unseen world and the there and then.

Within the context of casual exchanges, children can ask about an impressively wide range of topics—human behavior, the natural world, the customs of their communities, the inner lives of people they love, and the mysteries of social protocol. Take the following example, an exchange between a four-year-old and his father:

Child: You say, "Go away, dammit." Why you don't like the crows?

Father: Because the crows can get their own food.

Child: But why the chickens can't get their food too?

Father: Well, because we keep the chickens in a pen.

Child: But the crows are in the pen. You don't want those crows?

Father: Well, the crows can get into the pen, but we built the pen for the chickens because we take care of them. We like to eat their eggs.

Child: But we don't like crow eggs, right? Right, Dad? We like chicken eggs, right?

Notice that this is no simple exchange. The little boy seeks three kinds of information. He wants to know more about the rules that govern his father's behavior (why he doesn't like crows), differences between crows and chickens, and social norms (people take care of chickens, but not of crows, and eat chickens' eggs but not crows' eggs). In just seven dialogic turns, a rich array of interests is revealed and the little boy gets answers to several questions. He learns something.

In casual conversations like this one, children have a chance to let adults know what they don't understand and what they want to know more about. If an adult has the time and interest, it takes little skill or erudition to provide satisfying, helpful answers. Take the following exchange recorded by Gordon Wells (1986, 59):

James, age 5, comes into the kitchen just as his mother has taken some cakes out of the oven. There is a loud, metallic "Crack."

James: Who did that?

Mother: I expect it was the tin contracting.

James: Which tin?

Mother: The one with your pasty in.

James: Why did it make that noise?

Mother: Well, when it was in the oven, it got very hot and stretched a bit. I've just taken it out of the oven, and it's cooling down very quickly, you see, and that noise happens when it gets smaller again and goes back to its ordinary shape.

James: Oh! Was it a different shape in the oven?

Mother: Not very different. Just a little bigger.

James: Naughty little tin. You might get smacked if you do it again.

In this one brief exchange the child makes five contributions, four of them questions. In each case, James' mother answers him in a straightforward, helpful way, providing just the kind of information he is seeking. Parents often answer their children not in a purposeful effort to impart information (one gets no sense that James' mother set out to teach James about the impact of temperature changes on metal), but rather from an interest in relationship. They just want to talk to their children.

This observation may explain the discouraging finding researchers have uncovered when they've examined conversations in the classroom. The rate, length, and richness of adult-child conversations drop precipitously when children go to school. Obviously, the parent of even several kids has more time to talk than the teacher working with twenty or more children at a time. However, as conversation dwindles, so do opportunities to ask questions.

British psychologists Tizard and Hughes (2008) found that children asked as many as twenty-six questions an hour at home, but when those same children were recorded in school, the number dropped to two questions an hour. Nor does the picture get much better as children move through the grades. In fact, some research suggests that the amount of conversation wanes in direct proportion to an increase in formal learning tasks.

Yet questions are just as powerful a tool for learning after children enter school as they were before.

School-age children ask questions to acquire new information about the natural and social world, to find out what the people around them think and how they feel, to probe the logic of someone's argument, and to seek evidence for another person's claim. One might argue that questions provide a window into the child's expanding knowledge.

School-age children ask questions to acquire new information about the natural and social world, to find out what the people around them think and how they feel, to probe the logic of someone's argument, and to seek evidence for another person's claim. One might argue that questions provide a window into the child's expanding knowledge. Consider some of the questions I have recorded children asking as I observed in classrooms:

> Six-year-old girl: Who makes the calendar? Who decides, um, who is it that gets to . . . how come Christmas and Chanukah are always at the same time?
>
> Nine-year-old boy: I've been thinking. Is it really true that we all come from the same person? My brother told me we all have the same mom, named Lucy. Is that true?
>
> Ten-year-old boy: Why do we always sit in a circle when we're gonna talk about books?

These examples suggest the wide range of phenomena and information that pique children's interest: the relationship between religions, human evolution, and the rationale behind classroom rules. In each case, an attentive adult had the opportunity to provide information the child would value (and therefore probably retain) and also to learn something about what that student really wanted to know.

But questions like these rarely come out of the blue. They emerge in the meandering flow of conversation. The richer the conversational fabric of the classroom, the more likely children are to pose meaningful questions and to persist in gaining meaningful answers. Consider the following exchange:

Teacher: Jamie, I love those bright hats you always wear. Do you wear them because you're cold, or do you just like to be fashionable?

Jamie: *(age nine)* Yeah.

Teacher: Mmm, a fashionista, I see. [*Chuckles.*] I think we all like to show who we are by what we wear. Don't you?

Jamie: Yeah. What do you wear to show who you are?

Teacher: Oh, good question. I guess I wear sneakers and sweatshirts—you know, sporty clothes.

Jamie: So is that who you are? A sporty person?

Teacher: Yeah, I am, I guess. But not always. Sometimes I dress up. I do have a life outside of school.

Jamie: I wonder what it's like in places where everybody has to wear the same clothes. My father says everyone in North Korea dresses the same. Do you think that means they all have the same personality?

This conversation goes from idle chatter to a rich avenue of exploration that touches on cultural differences, the relationship between clothing and personality, and assumptions about North Korea. The context for Jamie's probing question is the teacher's seemingly idle chat about his hats. It takes eight turns to get there. The teacher shows a genuine interest in Jamie as well as a genuine interest in continuing the conversation. What happens next in this conversation is equally important.

Teacher: Gee, really? Maybe your dad is right. I'm not sure, though. We could look it up. Maybe you can find some pictures of people in North Korea. But that wouldn't tell us about their personalities, I guess, would it? I wonder how we'd find that out?

The teacher uses the student's question as a jumping-off point for a deeper level of analysis, raising the issue of how we can find out things we want to know.

Yet researchers have found that teachers don't always exploit the questions that emerge in such casual conversations to their fullest educational potential. Consider the following example from Gordon Wells' (1986, 88) data:

Lee: I want to show it to you.

Teacher: It's big, isn't it? What is it?

Lee: A conker [the nut of a horse chestnut tree].

Teacher: Yes.

Lee: Then that'll need opening up.

Teacher: It needs opening up. What does it need opening up for?

Lee: 'Cause the seed's inside.

Teacher: Yes, very good. What will the seed grow into?

Lee: A conker.

Teacher: No, it won't grow into a conker. It'll grow into a sort of tree, won't it? Can you remember the—

Lee: Horse chestnut.

Teacher: Horse chestnut, good. Put your conker on the nature table, then.

In this exchange, most of the questions come from the teacher. The conversation quickly becomes a chance for the teacher to test Lee's knowledge and to correct misinformation. My own observational data suggest that this kind of exchange is common. Teachers' questions are often aimed at getting the student to demonstrate his knowledge, rather than to engage in a chat that's interesting to both parties. But it needn't unfold that way. Contrast a similar example, drawn from my own observational data, in which there is a more mutual, authentic exchange:

Colm: *(age eight)* Mr. Daniels, I want to tell you something. Look. I brought in a snake skin.

Teacher: Ugh. I'm actually terrified of snakes. But that's cool, Colm. Where'd you find it?

Colm: Outside. I was walking to the bus stop. Look. I think those are rattles. Are those rattles?

Teacher: I don't really know. I don't really want to get too close.

Colm: But why are you are afraid? It's dead. You're afraid of dead things?

Teacher: Of snakes. I really don't like snakes. Even when they're dead. You know, there are lots of stories about why people are afraid of snakes. Some of them are really interesting. I'm not the only one afraid of snakes.

Colm: Not me.

Teacher: Yes, but it's a common fear. What are you afraid of?

When two people are equally interested in talking to one another, as Colm and his teacher are in this conversation, they cover a lot of ground. Both speakers offer several invitations for further inquiry and thought. Instead of using the quiz model captured in the previous example, the teacher here uses the exchange to broaden Colm's horizons. He links his own reactions to literature that is about the human fear of snakes. Colm gets access to a body of literature he might not know about, and he learns that, through books, people can connect their own immediate experience to the lives of other people. This spontaneous exchange about a snake's skin provides hefty academic lessons.

The Last Straw

Audrey had kept her worries at bay by focusing on the school's obvious success at teaching kids valuable academic skills. After all, maybe it was pie-in-the-sky to worry about whether the kids could be themselves or felt at home, in school, when the real point was to teach them to read, do math, and participate in school routines. But when it finally became clear that though they were learning reading skills, they weren't becoming readers, something in her shifted.

In March, Audrey told the administration she would be leaving the school at the end of the year. When they asked her why, she said, "I admire the way you are teaching the children to behave well. I can see that they are acquiring important tools here. But I need to work in a school where children can be children."

Epilogue

Child Development:
A User's Manual

———————◆———————

THINKING ABOUT YOUR students through a developmental lens will enhance your teaching each and every day. It will also make your job more interesting and therefore more fun. You can do this in a general way by getting into a three-step habit: First, try to notice small things that you hadn't noticed before—the specific things your students do and say. Then try to see what story all those small details and brief stretches of behavior are telling you about that particular child (or group of children). Finally, place what you've noticed or paid attention to within the context of a line of research or strand of developmental psychology that seems most relevant or that will help you make sense of whatever perplexes you about the child or the situation. Don't rush to decide which aspect of developmental psychology seems relevant. Sometimes it's not as obvious as it might seem. Let your mind wander a bit as you try to identify which particular strands of psychological development might illuminate the child or teaching puzzle you are thinking about.

We often underestimate the power of simply thinking differently about children —who they each are and the processes that brought them to this particular point in their lives. But thinking through the particulars about a given child is only a first step. Then you need to think about that child in terms of what scientific research tells us about how children, in general, develop. You need to look behind the scenes. Another way to think about this is to imagine that you could draw the child in question on a transparent sheet, showing in some graphic way whatever strength, weakness, or mystery about her was puzzling you. Now imagine you could place that sheet on a background of all we know about the particular developmental processes that seem relevant (a child who has trouble with others placed on a background sheet about how social relationships develop, for instance). Suddenly, the particular quirks or behaviors that had mystified you would make sense because they'd be amplified and fleshed out by the information in the background. Sometimes you'd have to place the sheet on different backgrounds to see which one best explained or illuminated the picture.

A developmental perspective rests on specific facts and data. But, like all science, knowledge about children changes as we acquire new scientific methods. Sometimes a new method allows us to gather data we've never had access to before (we now can measure the response of babies to novelty, for instance, by measuring their skin moisture and heart rate and the level of stress hormone they produce under various situations). Sometimes researchers at different labs, using a wide range of techniques, find that their data, taken together, upend some old way of thinking and reveal a better, more accurate way of thinking about a particular process. Doctors need to keep reading scientific journals to stay current with new advances in medicine. So, too, educators (even those who recently took a course in child development) need to keep updating what they know.

And yet, a developmental perspective is also a basic mind-set about education and children. People with this mind-set tend to see every child or learning situation in terms of underlying psychological processes: how and why people change over time. Acquiring this mind-set will transform your teaching.

If you want to make child development integral to your daily work with children, there are four concrete steps you can take:

1. *Become a developmental sleuth (or think like a researcher).* Thinking about your students from a developmental perspective can and should be a part of your approach to children all of the time. But it is particularly valuable when you are working with a child who perplexes you in any way or a classroom dynamic that catches your attention or troubles you (*managing* such dynamics is not enough; the goal is to use the classroom as a setting for helping children grow intellectually and personally, not just for keeping them orderly). Finally, if you have any hunch at all that a curriculum you are using is not leading your students to genuine intellectual transformation, or that they are learning specific information and procedures, but not developing new dispositions and ways of thinking, this too might be a reason to become a developmental sleuth.

2. *Collect data.* Here are four ways you can collect data:
   • *Keep a journal.* Your journal entries can focus on one child, a group of children, an activity, or a part of the room that for some reason has attracted

your attention. Record at least one entry every day for a week. You can jot down short notes throughout the day or just write one entry each day. Try to describe what you saw without interpreting or judging. Try to keep evaluative terms like *good, nice, smart, rude,* and *bad* out of the entries. Instead of writing, "Julia was great today," write, "Julia played for twenty minutes at the sand table. She had a frown on her face the whole time but never looked up once. After about five minutes, Maria joined her. Julia didn't talk to Maria, but they worked on the same pile castle." Note your feelings and reactions separately. "Marty threw his math book across the room today after he found out he got a 33 on the quiz. He drives me crazy sometimes." Don't read your entries until you have finished the journal (you may decide that a week is not enough and that you want to keep it for several weeks before going over it or taking any further steps).

- *Decide on one or more behaviors you want to keep a record of.* Choose a behavior that will help you understand something that is puzzling you. Make a chart or table with which to keep your record. For instance, imagine you are concerned that children aren't as interested in reading as you had hoped. You aren't sure why, and you are interested in figuring out what might lead them to more spontaneous independent reading. You might begin to figure out what is going on by keeping track of all the times children in your class read outside the scheduled reading periods. Your chart might look like the following one (in this table, each *x* represents an individual child who was reading a sentence, a paragraph, or a part of a book, from any source, in that space or during that time of day).

Areas of Room	Math Time	Social Studies	Lunch	Projects
Reading Corner		x x x x x	x	x x x x
Science Bench			x x x x x x	x x x x x x
Worktables	x x x x x x x x x			x

- *Write a full reflection on a particular child, activity, or part of the curriculum.* In this version, you write down everything you can think of about that child or activity. You might begin by describing the child and then go on to include every piece of information you can think of about her. What she looks like; what you know about her family; what interests, worries, delights, or saddens her. What she is good at and what she struggles with. How she approaches various activities. Imagine she is a character in a novel you are writing. You might also include a description here of how you think she would describe one whole day—what the classroom looks and feels like to her.

- *Talk to your students.* This should be the most obvious, and easiest, way to collect data but it's often overlooked in the hustle-bustle of a busy classroom. For a remarkable amount of the time that adults speak to kids in schools, they are either telling them something (new information, where to go next, how to do an assignment, or rules of some sort) or asking them a question to assess what they know (what I have elsewhere called the quiz model of conversation). But there are two kinds of talk that don't happen enough in classrooms. One is the kind of open-ended and rambling conversation we have with friends and family—a genuine exchange of ideas, experiences, and opinions. Why do I include this in a paragraph about gathering data? Because one of the best ways to learn about someone is to engage in a genuine conversation with her. Every good interviewer and therapist knows that. The second type of talk that can also be useful is asking a child a question about what he thinks and feels. Kids often have a lot to say and know more than you might think about what they need, educationally speaking.

3. *Reflect on your data.* Once you have some data, it's time to sit down and see what it can tell you. Let it surprise you. Children may be reading more (or less) than you think. A little boy you think of as quarrelsome may in fact be fighting with only one particular other child. One of the best uses of records is to discover a clue about what's going on with a child. For instance, if you have a student who seems to frequently lose control, you might keep a record of all the times she gets angry or distraught for two weeks. For each time you note an explosion, you might note down what time of day it is, what else is going on, and who else is with her. A careful look at that record might show you that she always loses control right before the class embarks on one of the topics that you know is difficult for her. Or to the contrary, you might find that she acts up when very little is going on. Your interpretation about what her outbursts mean, and therefore what you can do about them, will be different depending on what you learn from your observations and records.

   Perhaps you don't know what your data are telling you. Then it's a good time to read more about children's development. Ask yourself what you think you know about the aspect of development you're focusing on (for instance, differences between boys and girls in the way they make friends or the role of culture in mathematical knowledge). Write it down, so you can find out what you don't know and see which of your "facts" might actually just be conventional wisdom. Even if you don't have books or journals in your library, you can find almost anything on the Internet via Google Scholar. As you look through suggested titles, you'll get a sense of what kinds of research are being done, and this will expand your understanding in and of itself. Look for information, *not* techniques, suggestions, or plans. If you have a group of five-year-olds who fight all of the time, read about peer relations in early childhood. If you are worried that children in your third-grade class aren't learning to think well, find some new research on intellectual development in middle childhood. Read the studies themselves, so that you have some sense of how researchers arrived at the conclusions. And read a review so you get the big picture. Pick something written by a researcher, so that you get a scientific overview of recent advances in basic sciences, rather than the particular approach one educational philosophy or teacher wants to advocate for. Don't worry if the research doesn't instantly address your question or, better yet, if you find a few studies that disagree with one another. The goal is not to find, nestled in the literature, a simple concrete solution to your problem. The goal is to gain a more textured or fuller sense of how children develop, because that is the best route to knowing what is and isn't a real problem, when the problem lies in the child, and when it lies in your expectations. Getting a fuller sense of how children develop is the best way to devise your own solution to your own specific situation. This will always work better than using a prepackaged solution.

4. *Take action.* The whole idea of this book is that before you can fix a problem with something or someone in your classroom, you should step back and try to understand what's going on—really understand the underlying issues and the path(s) that led to the current situation. That kind of understanding requires more than just a few moments of reflection. It requires close description, record keeping, counting (behaviors, words, responses), and reading about topics in child development. Once you have new data and new information, you will probably arrive at a new way of thinking about what is going on or what needs to change. Each story in this book begins with a problem of some sort. But each ends with a solution of sorts. Sometimes the solution is simply to accept that a child is fine as he or she is. Another solution is to change how or what you teach. None of the solutions is very complicated or technical. But they all work in particular situations, and the

reason for that is fairly simple. They are each based on an understanding of developmental psychology—a clear idea about how a child got to be the way he or she is, how particular abilities unfold, and how to think about the processes of learning and development. In each case, the solution is quirky and specific to that situation.

In most cases, helping a child learn, fixing something that has stalled in your classroom, or opening up new possibilities for your group of students is fairly easy, once you really understand what's going on. Teachers are, in this way, not like doctors. Once doctors have reached a diagnosis, in most cases, there are just a few specific medical or surgical options they can recommend. However, teaching requires you to be inventive and flexible. You are the doctor, the medicine, and the procedure. But that's less onerous and overwhelming than it sounds, because once you've really understood what is going on, most solutions are low-key and available to you right there in the classroom.

Guidelines for Making Changes

Whenever possible, as you come up with new activities or plan some curriculum, build on children's natural inclinations; don't work against them. For example, rather than find a way to insist or cajole children into sitting still, come up with learning activities that employ their huge need to be active, both physically and mentally.

Think of ways for children to help each other, instead of keeping them separate. Children are, by and large, social creatures. And the process of development is, intrinsically, an interactive and social one.

Children are as quirky as adults. Don't try to make them all the same. A child who needs time alone, or has one very intense interest, should be helped to use his or her idiosyncrasy, not required over and over again to bypass or suppress it. We don't want all children to be the same. We want them to be more of who they each are.

Helping children learn or practice specific academic skills can be helpful, and sometimes it's required for one reason or another. But it's not the same as helping children develop. Make sure that, during the week, there are many opportunities for your children to develop new ways of thinking and being in the world. This is almost never a quick or efficient process, the way that learning a new skill might be. It may take a while to see the impact. But this is where research can give you confidence.

If good, current research has shown that a certain activity supports your students' development, stick with it, even if it doesn't immediately lead to higher test scores.

Most of all, feel free to be inventive and creative and to improvise when you are coming up with solutions to problems. This book contains several examples of teachers hitting upon a small change suited to a specific dilemma. If the small change, however quirky, grows out of observation, conversation, and careful thought about the particular child, or the nature of development, it is likely to have a big impact.

Finally, don't feel you can fix everything about a child. Your classroom is an environment rich with human interaction, which should foster a child's intellectual and personal growth. It's not an extrusion factory. So focus on how to make it a good environment for a child's development. Allow yourself to do a little less and notice a little more.

If I had to boil this advice down to a few sentences it would be these: Watch and listen to your students, and use what you see and hear to think about who they each are and how they are developing. Let those insights guide you as you come up with simple and low-key ways to help them grow.

References

Ainsworth, Mary D. Salter, Mary C. Blehar, Everett Waters, and Sally N. Wall. 2015. *Patterns of Attachment: A Psychological Study of the Strange Situation.* Abingdon, UK: Psychology Press.

Aronson, Elliot. 1997. *The Jigsaw Classroom: Building Cooperation in the Classroom.* Glenview, IL: Scott Foresman.

Asher, Steven R., and John D. Coie, eds. 1990. *Peer Rejection in Childhood.* Cambridge, UK: Cambridge University Press.

Asher, Steven R., and Shelley Hymel. 1986. "Coaching in Social Skills for Children Who Lack Friends in School." *Children and Schools* 8 (4): 205–218.

Asher, Steven R., and Valerie A. Wheeler. 1985. "Children's Loneliness: A Comparison of Rejected and Neglected Peer Status." *Journal of Consulting and Clinical Psychology* 53 (4): 500-505.

Baumrind, Diana. 1967. "Child Care Practices Anteceding Three Patterns of Preschool Behavior." *Genetic Psychology Monographs* 75 (1): 43–88.

____. 1989. "Rearing Competent Children." In *Child Development Today and Tomorrow*, ed. William Damon, 349–378. San Francisco: Jossey-Bass.

Bierman, K., & Furman, W. 1984. "The Effects of Social Skills Training and Peer Involvement on the Social Adjustment of Preadolescents." *Child Development* 55 (1), 151-162. doi:10.2307/1129841.

Blatchford, Peter, Anthony D. Pellegrini, and Ed Baines. 2015. *The Child at School: Interactions with Peers and Teachers.* Abingdon, UK: Routledge.

Bodrova, Elena, and Deborah J. Leong. 2007. *Tools of the Mind: The Vygotskian Approach to Early Childhood Education.* Columbus, OH: Pearson.

Bornstein, Marc H. 2002. "Parenting Infants." In *Children and Parenting*, vol. 1 of *Handbook of Parenting*, ed. Marc Bornstein, 3–43. Mahwah, NJ: Lawrence Erlbaum.

Bowlby, John. 1972. *Attachment.* Vol. 1 of *Attachment and Loss.* New York: Penguin Books.

Brown, Ann L. 1997. "Transforming Schools into Communities of Thinking and Learning About Serious Matters." *American Psychologist* 52 (4): 399–413.

Bruner, Jerome S. 1966. *Toward a Theory of Instruction*. Vol. 59. Cambridge, MA: Harvard University Press.

Burchinal, Margaret R., Ellen Peisner-Feinberg, Donna M. Bryant, and Richard Clifford. 2000. "Children's Social and Cognitive Development and Child-Care Quality: Testing for Differential Associations Related to Poverty, Gender, or Ethnicity." *Applied Developmental Science* 4 (3): 149–165.

Chess, Stella, Alexander Thomas, and Herbert G. Birch. 1965. *Your Child Is a Person: A Psychological Approach to Parenthood Without Guilt*. New York: Viking.

Coie, John D., Kenneth A. Dodge, and Heide Coppotelli. 1982. "Dimensions and Types of Social Status: A Cross-Age Perspective." *Developmental Psychology* 18 (4): 557–570.

Craig, Wendy M., and Debra J. Pepler. 1998. "Observations of Bullying and Victimization in the School Yard." *Canadian Journal of School Psychology* 13 (2): 41–59.

Crick, Nicki R., Juan F. Casas, and Monique Mosher. 1997. "Relational and Overt Aggression in Preschool." *Developmental Psychology* 33 (4): 579–588.

Delpit, Lisa. 2006. *Other People's Children: Cultural Conflict in the Classroom*. New York: New Press.

Deveaux, Alexis. 1991. *An Enchanted Hair Tale*. New York: HarperCollins.

Diamond, Adele, and Kathleen Lee. 2011. "Interventions Shown to Aid Executive Function Development in Children 4 to 12 Years Old." *Science* 333 (6045): 959–964.

Donaldson, Margaret. 1979. *Children's Minds*. New York: W. W. Norton.

Duckworth, Angela L., and Martin E. Seligman. 2005. "Self-Discipline Outdoes IQ in Predicting Academic Performance of Adolescents." *Psychological Science* 16 (12): 939–944.

Dunn, Judy. 2004. *Children's Friendships: The Beginnings of Intimacy*. Hoboken, NJ: Blackwell.

Eisenberg, Nancy, Richard A. Fabes, Jane Bernzweig, Mariss Karbon, Rick Poulin, and Laura Hanish. 1993. "The Relations of Emotionality and Regulation to Preschoolers' Social Skills and Sociometric Status." *Child Development* 64 (5): 1418–1438.

Engel, Susan. 1995. *The Stories Children Tell: Making Sense of the Narratives of Childhood*. New York: W. H. Freeman.

Evans, Angela D., and Kang Lee. 2013. "Emergence of Lying in Very Young Children." *Developmental Psychology* 49 (10): 1958–1963.

Fisher, Kelly, Kathryn Hirsh-Pasek, Roberta M. Golinkoff, Dorothy G. Singer, and Laura Berk. 2011. "Playing Around in School: Implications for Learning and Educational Policy." In *The Oxford Handbook of the Development of Play*, ed. Peter Nathan and Anthony D. Pellegrini, 341–360. New York: Oxford University Press. www.oxfordhandbooks.com/view/10.1093/oxfordhb /9780195393002.001.0001/oxfordhb-9780195393002-e-025.

Flynn, Emma Grace, and Andrew Whiten. 2010. "Studying Children's Social Learning Experimentally 'in the Wild.'" *Learning and Behavior* 38 (3): 284–296.

Fox, N. A., H. A. Henderson, K. H. Rubin, S. D. Calkins and L. A. Schmidt. 2001. "Continuity and Discontinuity of Behavioral Inhibition and Exuberance: Psychophysiological and Behavioral Influences across the First Four Years of Life." *Child Development* 72: 1-21. DOI:10.1111/1467-8624.00262.

French, Doran C., Xinyin Chen, Janet Chung, Miao Li, Huichang Chen, and Dan Li. 2011. "Four Children and One Toy: Chinese and Canadian Children Faced with Potential Conflict over a Limited Resource." *Child Development* 82 (3): 830–841.

Galen, Britt R., and Marion K. Underwood. 1997. "A Developmental Investigation of Social Aggression Among Children." *Developmental Psychology* 33 (4): 589–600.

Gawande, Atul. 2008. *Better: A Surgeon's Notes on an Imperfect Science*. New York: Picador.

Gopnik, Alison, Andrew N. Meltzoff, and Patricia K. Kuhl. 1999. *The Scientist in the Crib: What Early Learning Tells Us About the Mind*. New York: William Morrow Paperbacks.

Greenfield, P. 1984. "A Theory of the Teacher in the Learning Activities of Everyday Life." In *Everyday Cognition: Its Development in Social Context*, ed. by Rogoff and Lave. Cambridge MA: Harvard University Press.

Halliday, Michael A. K. 1973. *Explorations in the Functions of Language*. London: Edward Arnold.

Harris, Paul L. 2000. *The Work of the Imagination*. Hoboken, NJ: Blackwell.

____. 2012. *Trusting What You're Told: How Children Learn from Others*. Cambridge, MA: Harvard University Press.

Hart, Betty, and Todd R. Risley. 1995. *Meaningful Differences in the Everyday Experience of Young American Children*. Baltimore, MD: Paul H. Brookes.

Istomina, Z. M. 1975. "The Development of Voluntary Memory in Preschool-Age Children." *Soviet Psychology* 13 (4): 5–64.

Jensen, Arthur. 1969. "How Much Can We Boost IQ and Scholastic Achievement?" *Harvard Educational Review* 39 (1): 1–123.

Kagan, Jerome, and Nancy Snidman. 2009. *The Long Shadow of Temperament*. Cambridge, MA: Harvard University Press.

Lepper, Mark R., and David Greene, eds. 1978. *The Hidden Costs of Reward: New Perspectives on the Psychology of Human Motivation*. New York: Psychology Press/LEA.

Lewis, Michael, and Douglas Ramsay. 2004. "Development of Self-Recognition, Personal Pronoun Use, and Pretend Play During the 2nd Year." *Child Development* 75 (6): 1821–1831.

Lillard, Angeline S. 2016. *Montessori: The Science Behind the Genius*. Oxford, UK: Oxford University Press.

Lillard, Angeline S., Ashley M. Pinkham, and Eric Smith. 2011. "Pretend Play and Cognitive Development." In *The Wiley-Blackwell Handbook of Childhood Cognitive Development*, 2d edition, ed. Usha Goswami, 285–311. Chichester, UK: John Wiley and Sons.

Lindgren, Astrid. 1950. *Pippi Longstocking*. New York: Viking.

Miller, George A. 1991. *The Science of Words*. New York: Scientific American Library.

Miller, Patricia H. 2002. *Theories of Developmental Psychology*. New York: Macmillan.

Mischel, Walter. 2014. *The Marshmallow Test: Understanding Self-Control and How to Master It*. New York: Random House.

Nelson, Katherine. 1998. *Language in Cognitive Development: The Emergence of the Mediated Mind*. Cambridge, UK: Cambridge University Press.

Olweus, Dan. 1994. "Bullying at School." In *Aggressive Behavior: Current Perspectives*, ed. L. Rowell Huesmann, 97–130. New York: Springer.

Paley, Vivian G. 2009. *You Can't Say You Can't Play*. Cambridge, MA: Harvard University Press.

Piaget, Jean. 1967. *The Child's Conception of the World*. Paterson, NJ: Littlefield, Adams.

Piaget, Jean, and Bärbel Inhelder. 1969. *The Psychology of the Child*. New York: Basic Books.

Plomin, Robert, Jerome Kagan, Robert N. Emde, J. Steven Reznick, Julia M. Braungart, JoAnn Robinson, Joseph Campos, Carolyn Zahn-Waxler, Robin Corley, David W. Fulker, and J. C. DeFries. 1993. "Genetic Change and Continuity from Fourteen to Twenty Months: The MacArthur Longitudinal Twin Study." *Child Development* 64 (5): 1354–1376. doi:10.1111/j.1467-8624 .1993.tb02957.x.

Plomin, Robert, and John C. Loehlin. 1989. "Direct and Indirect IQ Heritability Estimates: A Puzzle." *Behavior Genetics: An International Journal Devoted to Research in the Inheritance of Behavior* 19 (3): 331–342. https://doi. org/10.1007/BF01066162.

Raver, C. Cybele, Stephanie M. Jones, Christine P. Li-Grining, Fuhau Zhai, Kristen Bub, and Emily Pressler. 2011. "CSRP's Impact on Low-Income Preschoolers' Preacademic Skills: Self-Regulation as a Mediating Mechanism." *Child Development* 82 (1): 362–378.

Scribner, Sylvia. 1986. "Thinking in Action: Some Characteristics of Practical Thought." In *Practical Intelligence: Nature and Origins of Competence in the Everyday World*, ed. by Robert J. Sternberg and Richard K. Wagner, 13–30. Cambridge, UK: Cambridge University Press.

Shapiro, Lawrence. 2010. *Embodied Cognition*. Abingdon, UK: Routledge.

Shonkoff, Jack P., and Deborah A. Phillips, eds. 2000. *From Neurons to Neighborhoods: The Science of Early Childhood Development*. Washington, DC: National Academy Press.

Siegler, Robert S. 1998. *Emerging Minds: The Process of Change in Children's Thinking*. Oxford, UK: Oxford University Press.

Skinner, B.F. 1953. *Science and Human Behavior*. New York: Simon and Schuster.

Smith, Linda, and Michael Gasser. 2005. "The Development of Embodied Cognition: Six Lessons from Babies." *Artificial Life* 11 (1–2): 13–29.

Snow, Catherine E. 2010. "Academic Language and the Challenge of Reading for Learning About Science." *Science* 328 (5977): 450–452.

Stern, Daniel. 1977. *The First Relationship*. Cambridge MA: Harvard University Press.

Stevenson, Harold W., Shin-Ying Lee, Chuansheng Chen, James W. Stigler, Chen-Chin Hsu, Seiro Kitamura, and Giyoo Hatano. 1990. "Contexts of Achievement: A Study of American, Chinese, and Japanese Children." *Monographs of the Society for Research in Child Development* 55 (1–2): i, iii–vi, 1–119.

Tizard, Barbara, and Martin Hughes. 2008. *Young Children Learning*. New Jersey: John Wiley and Sons.

Tomasello, Michael. 2014. *A Natural History of Human Thinking*. Cambridge, MA: Harvard University Press.

Trevarthen, Colwyn, and Ken J. Aitken. 2001. "Infant Intersubjectivity: Research, Theory, and Clinical Applications." *The Journal of Child Psychology and Psychiatry and Allied Disciplines* 42 (1): 3–48.

Tyler, Anne. 1988. *Breathing Lessons*. New York: Alfred Knopf.

Underwood, Marion K. 2007. "Gender and Children's Friendships: Do Girls' and Boys' Friendships Constitute Different Peer Cultures, and What Are the Trade-Offs for Development?" *Merrill-Palmer Quarterly* 53 (3): 319–324.

Underwood, Marion K., Britt R. Galen, and Julie A. Paquette. 2001. "Top Ten Challenges for Understanding Gender and Aggression in Children: Why Can't We All Just Get Along?" *Social Development* 10 (2): 248–266.

Ursache, Alexandra, Clancy Blair, and C. Cybele Raver. 2012. "The Promotion of Self-Regulation as a Means of Enhancing School Readiness and Early Achievement in Children at Risk for School Failure." *Child Development Perspectives* 6 (2): 122–128.

Van den Berg, B., and T. Cillessen. 2015. "Peer Status and Classroom Seating Arrangements: A Social Relations Analysis." *Journal of Experimental Child Psychology* 130:19–34.

Vygotsky, Lev S. 1980. *Mind in Society: The Development of Higher Psychological Processes*. Cambridge, MA: Harvard University Press.

Watson, John. 1928. *Psychological Care of Infant and Child*. New York: W. W. Norton.

Wells, Gordon. 1986. *The Meaning Makers: Children Learning Language and Using Language to Learn*. Portsmouth, NH: Heinemann.

Werner, Heinz. 1948. *The Comparative Psychology of Mental Development*. London: Follett Books.

Wynn, Karen. 1998. "Psychological Foundations of Number: Numerical Competence in Human Infants." *Trends in Cognitive Sciences* 2 (8): 296–303.

Yeager, David S., and Carol S. Dweck. 2012. "Mindsets That Promote Resilience: When Students Believe That Personal Characteristics Can Be Developed." *Educational Psychologist* 47 (4): 302–314.

Zajonc, Robert B. 1968. "Attitudinal Effects of Mere Exposure." *Journal of Personality and Social Psychology* 9 (2): 1–27.

Zelazo, Philip D., Ulrich Mueller, Douglas Frye, Stuart Marcovitch, Gina Argitis, Janet J. Boseovski, Jackie K. Chiang, Donaya Hongwanishkul, Barbara V. Schuster, and Alexandra Sutherland. 2003. "The Development of Executive Function in Early Childhood: I. The Development of Executive Function." *Monographs of the Society for Research in Child Development* 68 (3): vii–137.